World Wine
EDUCATION

DiMaggio Washington
Certified Sommelier; Wine Professor and WSET Instructor

AuthorHouse™
1663 Liberty Drive
Bloomington, IN 47403
www.authorhouse.com
Phone: 1-800-839-8640

First published by AuthorHouse   9/8/2010

ISBN: 978-1-4490-9155-2 (sc)

Library of Congress Control Number: 2010910451

Printed in the United States of America
Bloomington, Indiana

This book is printed on acid-free paper.

authorHOUSE®

Table of Contents

Introduction

Author's comment: I would like to thank many of the Authors listed in my reference section. It has been from those individuals that have contributed to much of my studies as well as the use of their textbooks in my class room. As a Certified Sommelier and professor of wine for several colleges, it is my intention to produce a textbook that is conducive for the student or wine enthusiast that would like to make this their first real step into the world of wines. Observing how many students study, I have acted on creating a digested version of many textbooks to bring about a collective set of extracted notes that would appear as flash cards and noting taking sheets. This is a format of which most students study from for any given exam. This text will cover a broad understanding and education of the key and most notable wine regions of the world. It is <u>not</u> my intention to cover every single country or regions within a country. That level of coverage would be expected over a number of wine classes and numerous textbooks. However after a decade of lecturing and utilizing various textbooks in my classes it became obvious that a "student's textbook" is really needed. A textbook set to cover "not everything" but the leading countries, regions, varietals, wine laws, maps and history that would make the education of wine, cleaner, clearer and easier to understand. This textbook will focus on key material needed and expected for most wine exams, from the beginner, to intermediate, and even some part for Advance studies. From an academic approach this textbook will seriously provide the student preparing for the first two levels of the Court of Master Program and / or the WSET program with information that is essential to those exams. The following in this textbook is a collection of information in a note taking format that should make it easy to understand each country's most noted regions, grapes and wine laws. Please understand that I have stripped away many regions within each country in order to present areas that are most applicable to test or exams. I have also made clear note as to what areas you should strongly consider committing to memory. This will contribute to a much more active knowledge of wines.

Our basic studying habits are to read chapter by chapter extracting key phases, subject matter, dates, laws, etc and then create notes, or flash cards, and have that become the principal means of our studies. I have attempted to do this for the student. All the key informational areas are noted without necessarily inundating the student with a tremendous amount of text to read though, in order to find key note taking information. Many of the wine textbooks, often lose the student in the "Too much information to filter through" syndrome. I introduce key charts and tables with digested text to explain … At a very quick and easy pace "with or without" the guidance of a classroom Instructor.

~Dedication~

I would like to dedicate this book to all of my former students. You are the ones that have inspired much of this book, and I thank you so much for that. Over the years many of you have remained in touch through emails and many have become friends and closer friends. I don't believe any other instructor could have been so privileged by your devotion, Passion and friendship.

At the beginning of each country or wine region, there is an easy to read information pages "Fast Facts" with boxes designed to give quick insight to that particular wine region… indicating the regions or sub-regions of the area, the grapes associated with the region or sub-regions, the soils and or climate if unique or worthy of note, and the wine laws for that country, region(s), and / or sub-regions if there are unique or additional local wine laws. In addition, there are "commit to memory" boxes throughout to make note of what is recommended to literarily commit to memory for a more active knowledge of wine, based on typical test or exams given in most wine courses.

1) This Chart covers the key regions within that country for a quick "at a glance" reference. Each following chart will cover the sub-regions of that major region.

2) This Chart covers the key grapes within that region for a quick "at a glance" reference.

3) This Chart covers the wine laws pertaining to that country. Where they apply, region or sub-regions laws will be noted if different or in addition to the main country laws and regulations.

4) This Chart covers the key soil(s) and / or climate conditions if note worthy for the region.

5) This is the flag recommending you to "Commit to Memory" this information based on most wine exams.

1

KEY COMMUNES DISCUSSED
IN REGION:

2

GRAPES OF THAT REGION
RED   WHITE

3

QUALITY CONTROLS AND LAWS:

The levels of quality control and countrywide or
regional laws

4

Soil:

Climate:

5

Commit to Memory

Chapter 1

A Bit of History

Wine has been around for thousands of years. History shows strong evidence of wine dating back as far as 5000 BC around the Middle East (former Persia) maybe the best location of the point of origin to date. The source of the fruit for the wine was something other than grapes at the time, the use of "Dates" may have been the best source of fruit for wine during this era. Throughout history wine has appeared within the various cultures as a typical beverage, as a choice to replace the bacteria issues with water, within religious uses and ceremonies, in celebrations and social gatherings. Wine has been very much an integral part of civilization for centuries. At the same time others have viewed it in total opposition as the drink of sin and sinful acts. Prohibition is a prime example of that in the 1920's the United States as well as Australia with the "Temperance Moment". Many religious orders have embraced the drink, while other religious orders have condemned alcohol as pollution to the body. Having said that, our interest will be addressing the cultures over thousands of years who have produced this beverage and cultivated its growth; Egypt, Rome, Greece. Much of the proliferation of wine can be contributed through the various orders of Monks that promoted the growth, techniques and education of viticulture, matching type of vine to type of soil, growing condition and fermentation practices. The Romans are attributed with the development and use of the Trellis as well as offering a "god of wine" Bacchus. While others such as the Christian with sacramental offering as the blood of Christ. The point gained, is wine had indeed been a major factor in the lives of civilizations.

Chapter 2

Viticulture and Enology Information Page

VITICULTURE

- ❖ VINES
- ❖ BRIX (MEASUREMENT)
- ❖ CLIMATE
- ❖ CANE
- ❖ SOIL
- ❖ CANOPY
- ❖ PHYLLOXERA
- ❖ PRUNNING
- ❖ ROOTS
- ❖ ROOT STOCKS
- ❖ SHOOTS
- ❖ TRUNK
- ❖ TRELLISING
- ❖ WEED MANAGEMENT
- ❖ SPUR
- ❖ HYBRID and CLONES
- ❖ ORGANIC / BIODYNAMIC

ENOLOGY

- ❖ HARVESTING
- ❖ FERMENTATION
- ❖ CRUSH AND DESTEMMING
- ❖ TERMINOLOGY
  - ➢ MUST
  - ➢ PRESSING
  - ➢ POMACE
  - ➢ LEES
- ❖ YEAST
- ❖ GRAPES and WINE STYLES
- ❖ EQUIPMENT
  - ➢ STAINLESS STEEL
  - ➢ OAK BARRELS
- ❖ RACKING
- ❖ FILTERING
- ❖ FINING
- ❖ BOTTLE / AGING
- ❖ CORKS
- ❖ PACKAGING

Viticulture And Enology

➢ **What is wine and what makes a great wine?**
- The process of converting the sweet juice of the grape to alcohol and carbon dioxide, along with the quintessential components of the grape, soils, weather and viticulture / enology techniques to yields a liquid in a bottle that produces the enjoyment that brings us, to friends, family and social gatherings and this textbook.
- Is wine made in the winery or the vineyard? The answer would have to be both, either place can make and break the wine. You can make great wine if you have great fruit but you can't make great wine with not so great fruit. Even the best winemaker will struggle to make even good wine from just okay fruit. So with that many will strongly support that the wine is made in the vineyard.

Viticulture

Vines and Root stocks

There exist today approximately 5000 types of varietals, the main species used for wine is Vitis Vinifera; although other species exist such as Vitis Labrusca; Vitis Rotundifolia; Vitis Riparia; and Vitis Rupestris. **Vitis Vinifera is the key to the most successful wine producing species.** Vines may be grafted onto a rootstock independent of the varietal. The rootstock provides the interface to the soil, the nutrients from the soil, as well as the water supply.

➢ **Anatomy of a Vine**
- Roots
- Root Stock
- Trunk
- Cane / Spur
- Shoots
- Flowers / Fruit / Leaves

Hybrid * Crossing * Clones

There are several ways that a vine varietal may come to exist and several reasons for wanting a new type available. The following covers 3 ways of obtaining a varietal.

➢ **Hybrid-** is one way to create another varietal. This is the process of crossing two or more Vitis varietals. Marrying two separate species in order to gain the benefits of both.
- **Vitis Vinifera**
  - The so-called European or wine grape, indigenous in the Europe and Asia area. This is regarded as the best-know wine grapes.
- **Vitis Labrusca**
  - Native to northeastern North America. The Concord and Niagara are the two main offshoots of this species.

- **Vitis Riparia**
  - Native to northeastern North America. Also native to Siberia and China.
    - Also known as Vitis Vulpina the river bank grape
- **Vitis Rupestris**
  - Native to North America.
- **Vitis Rotundifolia**   BERLANDIERI
  - Native to the southern half of the United States

➤ **Crossing:**
Crossing occurs when reproduction takes place the natural way.
- The same species
- Hermaphrodite
  - That is to say the flower contain both male and female organs
- Sexual reproduction takes place when the anthers mature and release pollen.
  - The pollen in transported by the wind, and lands on the stigmas of other grape flowers.

➤ **Clones**
- Growing a plant from the cuttings.
  - Genetic instructions to be copied every time a new cell is created. Coping is very accurate.
  - Mistakes that can happen are knows as
    - Mutations (this can be a nature made occurrence)

➤ **Pruning (Canopy and Cane)**
- To restrict to vegetation and to concentrate the vigor of the vine into production of fruit.
- To control the leaf canopy
  - Optimum exposure
  - To Shade from the sun
  - To aerate
- To keep the vineyard tidy
  - Ease of work and harvest

➤ **Pruning (Fruit)**
- Wine grapes benefit from struggle. There is such a thing as too much of a good thing. Too much water, fertile soil, bunches of grapes and large grape berries.
  - Pruning fruit (or dropping fruit) is a term use and performed to eliminate the competition. Vines will compete for water and nutrients. Too much availability of everything will allow the vine to grow large berries and many clusters which basically distributes the energy to produce weaker and less intense fruit. By pruning or dropping fruit, the available sources are forced to the remaining, creating better fruit with concentration of sugars, intensity and flavors, with tiny berries and fewer clusters.
  - Smaller berries and fewer clusters:

  ◆ Produce better fruit for higher quality wines
- Larger berries and greater clusters:
  ◆ Produce lesser quality wines, typically for inexpensive bulk wines.

Vineyard Practice and Methodologies

➢ **Standard** or as most vineyards are planted today
- A large percentage of vineyards today are planted using one of several trellising system as mentioned.
- In addition many will control or manage their vineyards with the use of one or more chemical means.
  - Pesticides
  - Herbicides
  - Insecticides
  - Chemical Fertilizers

➢ **Organic**
- Mendocino County is the largest organic wine growing region in California and is a good example to review for organic wines with no sulfites added.
- Sulfites naturally occur on the skin of the grapes and will have some small percentage in wine.
- For people used to drinking wines with a lot of SO_2 (sulfur dioxide), these wines are going to taste different, "When you taste unsulfured wines, the bright, fruity flavors are not as enhanced and the earthier flavors do not come through as much."
- For people that are very sensitive to sulfites "Organic Wines" may be the better alternative.

➢ **Biodynamic**
- The practice of biodynamics in viticulture (grape growing) has become popular in recent years in several growing regions, including France, Switzerland, Italy, Austria, Germany, Australia, Chile, South Africa, Canada, and the United States. A number of very high-end, high-profile commercial growers have converted recently to biodynamic practices.
- Some grape growers who have adopted biodynamic methods claim to have achieved improvements in the health of their vineyards, specifically in the areas of biodiversity, soil fertility, crop nutrition, and pest, weed, and disease management.
  - A method of organic farming that has its basis in a spiritual world-view.
  - As a practical method of farming, biodynamics embodies the ideal of an increasing ecological self sufficiency just as with modern agro-ecology, but includes ethical spiritual considerations.
  - The Key to biodynamics farming is considering the farm as a whole living system. Meaning biodynamic farms are supposed to be closed, self-sustaining systems. Biodynamics farming takes into account the pattern of lunar and cosmic rhythms. In this holistic view, the soil is seen not simply as ground for plant growth, but as an organism in its own right. The use synthetic / chemical fertilizers, herbicides and

pesticides are thus a <u>no no</u> to biodynamic practitioners. Instead, they use a series of special preparations to enhance the life of the soil, which are applied at appropriate times in keeping with the rhythms of nature. Disease is something to be address in the same manner, correct system and you correct the potential disease and it will go away.

- Below are just a few examples of soil preparation in the development of "living soil".
- Cow manure fermented in a cow horn, which is then buried and over winters in the soil
- Ground quartz (silica) mixed with rain water and packed in a cow's horn, buried in spring and then dug up in autumn.
  - The following is an example of soil preparation for the development of living soil.
    - o Flower heads of yarrow fermented in a stag's bladder
    - o Stinging nettle tea
    - o Oak bark fermented in the skull of a domestic animal
    - o Flower heads of dandelion fermented in cow mesentery
    - o (The list continues and continues but will not be covered within this textbook). This is just an example to the extent of Biodynamic development practice.

➢ Heat Summation or Degree Days <u>(Maynard Amerine (1911-1998) and Albert Julius Winkler (1894-1989) created the UC Davis Heat Summation Scale)</u>.

- Heat Summation or Degree Days as it is called as well, was developed at UC Davis as a means of identifying the various regions in respect to the amount of sun "or lack of sun" that region received during the growing season of the vineyard. This identification was divided into 5 regions in increments of 500 degree days. The days are measured by days that exceed 50°F (above this is the temperature represents the grow or production of a vine, temperatures exceeding 90° the vine production shuts down, so there is approximately a 40° window of vine production). The growing season for most areas is from April 1ˢᵗ to October 31ˢᵗ. *10°C – 22°C*

Calculating a couple of examples:

Measuring a day in April for instance: The temperature low is 50°F, the high for that day (time within a 24 hour period) is 61°F, then the average temp for the day can be said to have been: 55.5°F. That is to say (50 + 61 divided by 2. Therefore 55.5°- 50° is 5.5 degree day. **Measuring a day in June for instance**: The temperature low is 60°F, the high for that day (time within a 24 hour period) is 81°F, then the average temp for the day can be said to have been: 70.5°F. That is (60 + 81 divided by 2). Therefore 70.5°- 50° is 20.5 degree day. This would continue for everyday for the entire growing season. Adding each day accumulating the degrees for a period of let's say 200 days, will produce "Degree days" near 2,500 to over 4,000 degree days.

- ❖ *The Use of the UC Davis Heat Summation Scale in California*
- ❖ REGION I   2500 days or less   The coolest region
- ❖ REGION II   2501 to 3000 days
- ❖ REGION III   3001 to 3500 days
- ❖ REGION IV   3501 to 4000 days
- ❖ REGION V   4001 days or greater   The warmest region

Components And Terminology

- ➢ **Brix or Brix degrees**
  - ▪ This is the term used to measure the sugar content or percentage as it develops in the grape berries and is the potential for producing alcohol as a result of the completion of the fermentation. Brix (pronounced "Bricks") is one method of measuring the sugar potential alcohol in the grape berry, in the <u>vineyard</u> or <u>laboratory</u> we typically use a refractometer device to accomplish this. This method uses index refraction of light to measure the angle of incoming light based on the level of sugar present. There are four basic or main types of refractometers: The traditional handheld type (non electronic with a pre-scaled index corresponding to unit levels of Brix); the digital handheld type; the laboratory type or Abbe refractometer; and the inline process refractormeter. Other unit measurements are Baumé Scale; Balling Scale; Specific Gravity Scale; and Oeschlé Scale.

- ➢ **Various means of measuring sugar level in the grape berry or Must**
  - ▪ **Baumé Scale** is named after the French Pharmacist (Antoine Baumé)
  - ▪ **Balling Scale** is named after a Czechoslovakian chemist.
  - ▪ **Brix Scale** (pronounced "Bricks") was created by a Austrian physicist and mathematician, as an improvement to the Balling Scale and probably the more used measurement scale in the United States.
  - ▪ **Specific Gravity** is based on units of hydrometry (indicating the relative density to water)
  - ▪ **Oeschlé** is name after its Swiss inventor, is directly related to Specific Gravity.

- ➢ **Climate:** the following are climate characteristics that should be committed to memory as you will find reference to these conditions throughout this textbook and others alike.
  - ▪ Maritime climate
    - • Characterize by warm summers and mid winters.
  - ▪ Mediterranean
    - • Maritime climate where most of the rainfall occu[...]   *Commit to Memory*
  - ▪ Continental
    - • In the middle of substantial landmass.
    - • Extreme temperatures in both winter and summer.

> **Soils Types**
>   - Sandy Soil
>   - Silt Soil
>   - Clay Soil
>   - Loamy Soil
>   - Chalky Soil
>   - Limestone Soil
>   - Calcareous Soil

Vineyard Management and Conditions

> **Canopy**
>   - This is a term used in reference to the leaves shading the growing fruit on the vine. Canes or shoots are allowed to grow and produce leaves that perform 2 key functions. One is the process of photosynthesis.
>   - Photosynthesis: is a process that converts Carbon dioxide into organic compounds, especially sugars (Fructose or Glucose), using the energy from sunlight.
>   - **six molecules of water plus six molecules of carbon dioxide produce one molecule of sugar plus six molecules of oxygen**
>   - $6H_2O + 6CO_2 \longrightarrow C_6H_{12}O_6 + 6O_2$
>   - Sugar: Grape juice is comprised of simple compounds, glucose and fructose. Thinking in term of table sugar => sucrose => is a molecule of glucose bonded to a molecule of fructose.
>   - The other is providing shade or shelter from extreme sunlight of mid day and other elements.

Weed Management

One way or another, weed abatement is necessary, especially immediately around the vine itself. Weeds will consume the available water supply, depriving the vines. As mentioned, many vineyards are managed by some use of herbicides this becomes something to avoid with Organic vineyards and a complete <u>no no</u> with Dynamic vineyards.

> Types of Herbicides
>   - Pre-emergence
>   - Applied to the soil before germination of the weed seed.
>   - Post-emergence
>   - Material that kills growing weeds.
> No one Herbicides kills all weeds
> Planted crops for weed suppression. A none herbicide effort is to encourage a ground media to promote a ground crop that prevents unwanted weeds or at least minimize the germination at the same time supply a harbor for insects that redirects their feeding interest. This is referred to as "Crop Cover". Just before the budding of the vines, tiling crop cover into the soil then provides nitrogen needed for the vines.

- ▪ Cover crop plants
  - • Live plant material as mulch to suppress
- ➢ Mechanical Management: physically pulling weeds out of the ground that are surrounding the vines by hand or hand tools. Tractors work great for the middle of the rows.
  - ▪ Physically removing weeds

Trellising

There are various types of trellising. Trellising is a means of supporting the vines as the weight of the fruit increases. Trellising also provides opportunity to train the vines in the direction and behavior desired. It provides support for the canopy and in many cases brings the fruit level at an ergonomic height for harvesting the fruits. Various trellising is used based on the zone or region of the vineyard, in some cases the type of varietal, the orientation of the vineyard in respect to the sun and or slope of the land. Some other considerations are, if the vineyard will be managed by use of tractor equipment or fully manual management. Machine versus manual will in many cases determine the spacing of the trellising between rows apart and vines apart. There are a number of typical plantings but examples would follow: patterns in feet of (5 x 5; 5 x 6, 6 x 6… etc). Tractors need space to negotiate between rows, as humans will require less distance apart between rows. The Cordon trained and bilateral trained vines are some of the most common trellis practice. Below is a list of the most common based vineyard expectations and location.

- • Head trained vines
- • Cordon trained (single system)
- • Bilateral Cordon trained
- • Geneva double curtain (downward)
- • Lyre or U systems
- • Scott Henry system
- • Cane or Spur pruning planned

Phylloxera 1863

- • These almost microscopic, pale yellow sap-sucking insects, related to aphids, feed on the roots and leaves of grapevines depending on the phylloxera genetic strain.
- • In the mid 1800's the phylloxera epidemic destroyed most of the vineyards in Europe, most notably in France. Phylloxera was introduced to Europe by means of hitch hiking on ship transportation. France was equally interested in the varietals known and available in America and during the events of returning to France with various specimens, inadvertently brought this louse with it. They continued many attempts until finally discovered that the American rootstock was Phylloxera resistant. Because phylloxera is native to North America, the native grape species there are pretty much resistant. By contrast, the European wine grape Vitis vinifera is very susceptible to the insect. The epidemic devastated vineyards, destroying most of the European wine growing industry. In 1863, the first vines began to deteriorate inexplicably in the southern Rhône region of France. The problem spread rapidly across the continent. Some estimate that 90% of all European vineyards were destroyed. Phylloxera since that time

has now devastated much of the world to one level or another. Very few areas now exist that remain untouched by phylloxera.

Enology

The Fermentation Process

➢ **Fermentation**
- This is a process of converting grape sugar by yeast to ethanol or (ethyl alcohol) and carbon dioxide.
  - ALCOHOL FERMENTATION PROCESS
    - $C_6H_{12}O_6 => 2C_2H_5OH + 2CO_2 + HEAT$
      - CO_2 (Carbon Dioxide) => is the gas byproduct of yeast consuming sugar.
      - Heat => being a biological function generated from the yeast consuming the sugar and producing ethanol and CO_2 as its byproduct.
➢ Yeast (Saccharomyces cerevisiae) basically sugar loving yeast.
- Yeast is a single cell organism. During the fermentation process, the yeast consumes the grape sugar; and continues to reproduce by splitting or dividing in a binary fashion with the byproduct being (ethanol). The are a number of different yeast stains, each producing a very different type of wine based on flavors, speed or duration time of fermentation and side characteristics that are associated with different yeast stains.
➢ Grapes: White and Red also called (black) see the list of grapes below as the typical and most common grapes used. Many grape varieties vary from country to country and may be very unique to that country or region.
➢ Equipment
- Tanks
  - Used to hold must during cold soak and fermentation. For white wines and some reds, the wine may remain completely in the stainless steel tank until bottled.
- Pumps
  - Used to transfer wine from one tank to another, used for pumping over; the process of mixing the cap with the juice to maintain skin contact and achieving greater extraction and complexity.
- Crusher – de-stemmer
  - This can be two separate pieces of equipment but typically one unit performing two operations. The removal of the stems and leaves from the cluster and slightly breaking the skin to start juice flow and exposure to yeast for fermentation.
- Press
  - There are a number of different types of press. One of the older styles is called a basket press. Looking much like a large basket with a turn style vice at the top that rotates on threads force a large circular wooden block down on the must forcing the juice out the sides. The first juice is called "Free Run", this is juice with far less tannins and skin extraction because the grape are not under mechanical press. Any force applied is typically due to just the weight of the must itself. As mechanical pressure is applied greater flow of juice occurs as well as greater extraction of tannins and color. After

pressing the solids, (skin, seeds, some pulp, some stems) make up to what is called (Pomace) a compressed cake, absent of all juice.

- ◆ The equipment mentioned are used as a must have standard equipment for most wineries to produce their product.
- ◆ The grapes are harvested, typically collected in bins (in some cases, the grapes are sorted for better quality) and then placed in a crusher / de-stemmer. This equipment performs two operations, one the removal of the stems and leaves from the cluster and then slightly breaking the skin to cause juice flow, but not to seriously macerate the grape. The breaking of the grape for juice flow is sufficient for fermentation to start. The output of this process produces what is called **_Must_**.
- ◆ The Stainless steel tanks are used to hold the **_Must_** (the juice, skins, seeds, pulp, and some stem possibly) after crush and de-stemming. The Must may go through a cold soak period of a day or so, with <u>sulfur dioxide</u> (this is typically in the form of a solid Potassium Metabisulfite) added as a preservative during this period and for most wine product a means to kill off the wild yeast from jump starting an undesired fermentation. The yeast (one or more can be selected from a list of strains based on the expected results of the wine maker) is then added (inoculation) to the Must and fermentation begins. The wine maker will monitor this process as the sugar is consumed by the yeast and alcohol raises in percentage. Fast math, we typically will calculate a 1 to .5 ratio, meaning for every one part sugar will produce .5 part alcohol. Therefore a Brix measure in the vineyard of let's say 24brix, would have a potential of 12% alcohol. Having said this, most yeast strain can be a bit more aggressive and yield conversion numbers higher. (For example a syrah type yeast of .57) doing the math here, the same brix harvest of 24 then becomes (24 x .57 = 13.68%, which is more realistic number. Based on yield strain, the range may vary from (.5 to .57 or .58). If the sugar levels are higher; 25 or more then one can potentially expect resulting alcohol levels in the high 14 or 15 percentile or a bit more. There are constraints, most yeast strains will die off from their own waste byproduct. When alcohol levels get too high the yeast can no longer survive. Refer to (**How it is made**) for the continuing wine making process. Each style requires a different process for the completed finish. Once the yeast consumes all the sugar, the food source is gone and the fermentation process ends. Malolatic fermentation may be utilized, (referenced later chapter).

- ➢ Temperatures:
  - ▪ The temperature is critical during the fermentation process. Nowadays we have the ability to regulate the temperature by use of stainless steel tanks that are double jacketed or (basically have two walls, and between the inner and outer wall a coolant is pumped through allowing the regulation of temperature. White wines are fermented at lower temperatures than red. This decision is made by the wine maker in respect to the type of wines he or she seeks. Cold fermentation allows for a fruitier, crisp clean type of mouth-feel with white wines and a greater extraction of color and richness with red wines.
- ➢ Stainless steel

- Stainless steel tanks are used due to their ability to resist staining, corrosion, rust and their ease of cleaning. Stainless steel only, gives a clean, crisp and unaltered fruit quality to the wine.

➢ Maturation
- This is the process of aging or maturing the wine for some period of time and under certain conditions based again on style and wine expectation. Wine can completely remain on stainless steel, and there are some advantages or characteristics obtained from doing that. Or the wine may go into oak barrels for additional maturing and certain aging characteristics from that, And can also received maturation from a period of time in the bottle itself.

➢ Fining
- Is a process that may or may not be used by the Winemaker. It is often used to remove tannins or lower astringency but mostly to remove microscopic particles that could cloud the wines.
- It is a method for extracting proteins from the wine. The process is a bonding effect whereas the protein source introduced bonds with the proteins present in the wine. Once bonded the weight of the two settles to the bottom of the tank or barrel and eventually racked off.
  - **Gelatin** has been used in winemaking for centuries and is a traditional method for wine fining.
  - Besides gelatin, other fining agents for wines are often derived from animal and fish products.
    - **Egg whites**
      - Is also pretty common and used throughout Europe and North America. This is added to the vat of wine, bonds with existing proteins, settles to the bottom and eventually racked off.
    - **Bull's blood**
      - This always gets the attention of students with a responding frown. This is more of past history, than present day but nevertheless at one point a method for clarifying wine.
    - **Isinglass** (Sturgeon bladder)
      - Another alternative for protein bonding.
    - PVPP (a dairy derivative protein)
- BENTONITE
  - Non-animal-based filtering agents, (a volcanic clay-based filter)
  - Diatomaceous Earth.

➢ Filtration
- This is a mechanical process much like the use of a water filter in the home or oil filter in the car. Paper filters and membrane filters (thin films of plastic polymer material) for removing solid particles from the wine.

Oak Barrels

Most cooperages tend to make wine barrels from white oak. White Oak meets the requirements of porosity, strength, resilience, workability, weight and character. The large thick rays of the wood give white oak extra toughness and bend ability, while making it relatively stable during dry shrinkage and wet swelling.

➤ **French**
  ▪ French Oak was once (and still is by many) considered the most desirable wood for making wine barrels. Most French Oak comes from one or more of the forests planted in the days of Napoleon for ship building. Five of those forests are primarily used for wine barrel making. Allier, Limousin, Nevers, Trancais and Vosges forests produce woods with distinctive characteristics and winemakers select their barrels based on the desired effect for the finished wine.

➤ **Hungarian**
  ▪ Hungarian Oak barrels are much like the traditional French Oak barrels from the aspect of flavor characteristics.
  ▪ Hungary's forests typically contain a mix of deciduous species rather than more single species plantings that can be found heavily managed forests. A mixed forest can still experience problems, but as a whole mixed forest is generally a healthier forest with lower disease and parasites.

➤ **American**
  ▪ French Oak in the past has been the Oak barrel of choice. It is now pretty common to find American Oak as well as that of several other countries including Hungary in the use of wine barrels. American Oak typically cost less nearly half the price of French Oak Barrels.
  ▪ American barrel are not typically distinguished by various forest as in France. Although American white oak forests has now expanded to 18 Eastern American states and Oregon. The major eastern forests primarily Arkansas for quite sometime but now range from Pennsylvania in the North East through North Carolina, Tennessee, Kentucky, Missouri and Mississippi in the south.
  ▪ There is always an interesting comparing between American oaked wines to French oaked wines. While both American and French oak contribute tannin and aroma, French oak contains more tannin and flavor components and has a less obviously "oaky" flavor and smell than American oak. American oak has a more of a mouth-feel and forward and direct aroma. American oak contains more vanilla aroma and you will often hear the term such as "Big Oaky California Wines".

Process of Bending the Barrel

➢ **Fired Bent**
- ▪ Fire bent barrels are made from an air dried process and slowly toasted over an oak fire, caramelizing the natural occurring sugars in the wood. **air dried American oak, leisurely toasted**

➢ **Water Bent**
- ▪ Water bent barrels are soaked in very hot water, then bent to shape, then slowly toasted over an oak wood fire while still wet. Water is a better conductor than air therefore the toasting reaches greater depth. The typical characteristics with the barrel are associated with a sweet nose, and "Baking Spices"; spicy vanilla, cinnamon, nutmeg and roast nut and typically a softer velvet like texture.

Toasting of the Barrels

Various degrees of toasting or charring the inside of the oak barrels. This process is achieved by placing a temporary framed oak barrel over an oak fire. The degree of toasting in typically specified by the winemaker or retailer ordering barrels.

- • Light Toasting (LT)
- • Medium Toasting (MT)
- • Heavy Toasting (HT)
- • The Heads of the barrels may or maybe not be toasted. This too may be specified.

Bottle Sizes

Bottles (sizes may vary dependent on (date, country, region and outside of Europe). Not all bottles exist for every region

- ▪ A **standard** wine bottle is 750 ml
- ▪ A **split** is (Champagne only) and is 187ml
- ▪ A **half** bottle is 375ml
- ▪ A **Magnum** is two standard wine bottle or 1.5 liters
- ▪ A **Double Magnum** is four standard bottle or 3 liters
- ▪ A **Jeroboam** is approximately 3 liters or four standard bottle or 3 liters
- ▪ A **Rehoboam** is 4.5 liters or 6 standard bottles
- ▪ A **Imperial** is 6.0 liters (Bordeaux only)
- ▪ A **Methusalem** is approximately 6 liters or 8 standard bottles
- ▪ A **Salmanazar** is 9 liters or equal to 12 standard bottles
- ▪ A **Balthaza**r is 12 liters or 16 standard bottles
- ▪ A **Nebuchadnezzar** is 12 – 16 liters or 16 – 20 standard bottle
  - • (dependent on date, country and or region of origin)
- ▪ A **Sovereign** is approximately 50 liters or 67 standard bottles

Major white grape varietals

Aligote	Chardonnay
Chenin Blanc	Pinot
Columbard	Gris/Grigio
Folle Blanche	Riesling
Gewurztraminer	Roussanne
Gruner Veltliner	Sauvignon
Malvasia	Blanc
Marsanne	Scheurebe
Melon de Bourgogne	Semillon
Muller-Thurgau	Sylvaner
Muscadelle	Trebbiano
Muscat	Ugni Blanc
Palomino	Verdicchio
Pedro Ximenez	Viognier
Pinot Blanc	

Major red grape varietals

Barbera	Nebbiolo
Brunello	Petit Sirah
Cabernet Franc	Petit Verdot
Carignan	Pinotage
Carmenere	Pinot Meunier
Cabernet Sauvignon	Pinot Noir
Cinsault	Sangiovese
Dolcetto	Syrah/Shiraz
Durif	Tempranillo
Gamay	Tinta Barroca
Grenache	Tinta Cão
Grignolin	Touriga
Malbec	Touriga
Merlot	Nacional
Montepulciano	Tinta Roriz
Mourvedre	Zinfandel

Wine Making Styles

- ➢ **What makes a great wine**
  - ▪ Varietal Character
  - ▪ Integration
  - ▪ Expressiveness
  - ▪ Complexity
  - ▪ Correctness

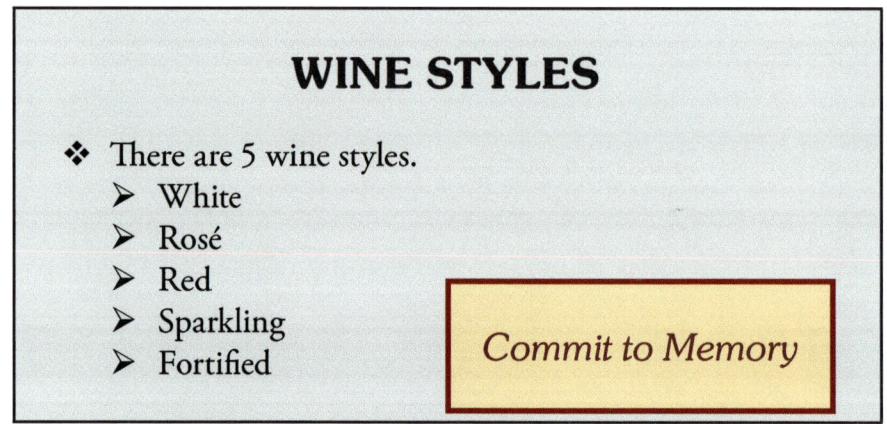

WINE STYLES

- ❖ There are 5 wine styles.
  - ➢ White
  - ➢ Rosé
  - ➢ Red
  - ➢ Sparkling
  - ➢ Fortified

Commit to Memory

Styles * Definition * Levels

- ➢ **White** (Reference White grape list)

- ➤ **Rosé**
  - ▪ Various degrees of skin contact time varying tint (color)
  - ▪ In some cases the tint is brought about by adding red wine to a white wine (rare)
- ➤ **Red** (Reference Red grape list)
- ➤ **Sparkling**
  - ▪ This includes: Sparkling wines in respect to country or regions for that style. Champagne has been the euphemism for all sparkling wine. Champagne is a key region in France and holds the title to the term Champagne. In respect to that other countries and regions have respected that and now indentify their sparkling wines as noted before. Even sparkling wine outside of the region of Champagne is giving another name, "Cre'mant". The following is a list of names for that country or regions sparkling wine.

  - ▪ Champagne (Region Only)
  - ▪ France - Cre'mant
  - ▪ Spain – Cava
  - ▪ Germany – Sekt / Deutscher Sekt
  - ▪ Italy – Spumante – Prosecco - Frizzante
  - ▪ South Africa – Cap Classic
  - ▪ California - Sparkling
- ➤ **Styles (Sweetness or Dryness) for Sparkling Wines**
  (Must producers will follow the level standard to Champagne Houses)
  - ▪ Brut Nature / Brut Zero / Ultra Brut = 0-2 g/l (not often used)

- • Extra Brut = very dry = 0 – 6 g/l
- • Brut = very dry to dry = 0 – 15 g/l
- • Extra – Sec / Extra dry = off dry = 12 – 20 g/l
- • Sec / Seco / Trocken = medium dry = 33-35 g/l
- • Demi Sec / Halbtrocken / Abbocato = 33 – 35 g/l
- • Deux / sweet / Dolce / Dulce / Luscious 50+ g/l

Champagne Styles

These are French terms use in Champagne and adopted by most regions producing a Sparkling wine style.

- ▪ Non – Vintage (NV)
- ▪ Vintage (Champagne is one of two wines that can actually hold a "Vintage" title. The other is Port).
- ▪ Prestige Cuvée
- ▪ Rosé
- ▪ Blanc de Noir (Pinot Noir / Pinot Meunier)

- Blanc de Blanc (Chardonnay only)

❖ **Non – Vintage** refers to a Champagne style where more than a single year of wine is blend in. Since the grapes come from multiple or at least not from one single year, a year can not be used on the bottle and therefore it is a "Non Vintage", occasionally you will see MV, indicating multiple years blended in. This does not reduce the quality of the wine, in fact, most Champagnes blend wines from more than one year.

❖ **Vintage** refers to a great year where the winemaker uses that year's grapes for the wine. In addition, a declared year must take place and 80% of those grapes must be use in that wine. Not ever year in a declared year, each Champagne house must make that decision.

❖ **Prestige Cuvée** refers to a proprietary blended wine (usually Champagne) that is considered to be the top of a producer's range.

❖ **Rosé** refers to one of the 5 wine styles as mention earlier, this is where the skins of the red grapes is left in contact with the Must long enough to exact color, causing a blush or pinking tint to the wine or in some cases a small amount of red wine is added to a white wine resulting in the same blush or tint color.

❖ **Blanc de Noirs** refers to the use of entirely red grapes to make a white wine. Blanc de Noir is "White of Blacks". In most grapes the juice of a grapes, white or red, the juice is white, there are just a very few grapes, where the juice is actually red. For Champagne, only two red grapes are allowed (Pinot Noir and Pinot Meunier)

❖ **Blanc de Blancs** refers to the use of only white grapes. "White of Whites" since there is only one white grape used for Champagne that implies "Chardonnay". The term is use by other areas where other white grapes are used.

Process steps for making Champagne

➢ **Secondary Fermentation**
A secondary fermentation; refers to the repeat of a fermentation process but this time in the bottle itself. Remember the fermentation process converts the sugar of the grape juice into Alcohol and Carbon Dioxide (CO_2), heat is also produce as a biological derivative of the yeast byproduct. But typically does not go into much consideration at this level.

- The Traditional Method is the inoculation of a French term called:
  - Liqueur de Tirage
    - This is a "Cocktail" of wine, sugar, yeast nutrients & clarifying agent
    - Riddling
      - Developed at the beginning of the 19th century by the widow "Veuve" Clicquot herself and chef de cave Antoine Müller.
  - Disgorgement refers to the process of removing the yeast sediment resulting from the secondary fermentation in bottle of Champagne and other quality sparkling wines.
  - The Transfer Method
    - To avoid high cost and complication of Traditional method
    - This process is done is large tanks and then the sparkling wine transferred into bottle avoiding the individual cost and effort associated with managing individual bottles and bottle variation of wine.

- CO2 Injection Method (not covered in this discussion)

➢ **Fortified**
- Port; Sherry; Madeira; Marsala (typical fortified wines)
- **Port Styles**
  - White – white grapes – off dry to sweet
  - Ruby – UK market – sweet - simple
  - Reserve Ruby - better Ruby ports – age 5 years
  - Tawny – blending Ruby and White Ports
  - Reserve Tawny
  - Tawny with an Indication of Age 5, 10, 15, 20, 25+
  - Crusted British specialty (unfiltered)
  - Late Bottled Vintage (LBV) (undeclared year)
  - Colheita - Portugal – single vintage – min 8 years
  - Vintage – Declared year – bottled when 2 years
    - Port is one of two wines that can hold the actually title of "Vintage".
  - Single Quinta Vintage – Single Estates

> *Commit to Memory*

➢ **Sherry Styles**
  - Fino -
  - Manzanilla
  - Amontillado
  - Palo Cortado
  - Oloroso
  - Pedro Ximenez (PX) 400 g/l
  - Cream
  - Pale Cream
➢ **Madeira Styles**
  - Finest / 3 year old
  - Reserve / 5 year old
  - Special Reserve / 10 year old
  - Extra Reserve / 15 year old
  - Vintage /noble grape / single vintage/ aged in oak for a min of 20 years
➢ **Other fortified Styles**
  - **Vin Doux Naturels**
    - High – Strength (95% abv) grape spirit is added to a partially fermented must to make a strong (15 – 20) % sweet wine.
      - Muscat VDNs
      - Grenache VDNs
  - **Marsala (grapes for this style)**
    - Cataratto, Grillo and Inzolia grapes
    - Ambra; Oro; Rubino

How are the 5 wine styles made?

- **White Wine process**
  - Harvesting the grapes
  - De-stemming and Crushing the grapes
  - Pressing the grapes
  - Fermenting the Juice of the grapes
- **Rosé Wine process**
  - Harvesting the grapes
  - De-stemming and Crushing the grapes
  - Fermenting the Must of the grapes
  - Limiting the amount of skin contact time of the Must
  - Pressing the grapes
- **Red Wine process**
  - Harvesting the grapes
  - De-stemming and Crushing the grapes
  - Fermenting the Must of the grapes
  - Pressing the grapes
- **Sparkling Wine process**
  - Harvesting the grapes
  - De-stemming and Crushing the grapes
  - Pressing the grapes
  - Fermenting the Juice of the grapes
  - Secondary fermentation to take place in the bottle
- **Fortified Wine process (Varies with type of fortified wine)**
  - Harvesting the grapes
  - De-stemming and Crushing the grapes
  - Fermenting the Must of the grapes
  - Pressing the grapes

➤ **PORT:** ferment to the level of residual sugar desired and then arrest the fermentation process by adding fortifier (clear / odorless Brandy) to the Must, stopping the fermentation process. The sweetness of the Port is a result of percentage of sugar residing in the Must at the time of adding the Brandy. The alcohol level is a result of alcohol converted by yeast prior to the fortification and the amount and strength of the Brandy (fortifier added) to the Must at the time of arresting the fermentation.

➤ **SHERRY:** ferment the Must completely and then add fortifier (clear / odorless Brandy) to the Must, after the fermentation is complete. The sweetness of the Sherry is a result of percentage of sugar added after fermentation. The alcohol level is a result of alcohol converted by yeast prior to the fortification and the amount and strength of the Brandy (fortifier added) to the Must at the time fermentation is completed.

Commit to Memory

➢ **Madeira** is a fortified wine made in the Madeira Islands. The wine can vary in style from very dry to incredibly sweet. There are four grapes from which the Madeira is produced. Like Port and other fortified wines, Madeira was a standard for ports of call. The use of brandy to fortify the wine like Port or Sherry prevents the wine from spoiling during long voyages. Water was not the beverage of choice because of the susceptibly to bacteria. One of the benefits of wine is that no human pathogen survives. The addition of brandy offered an even greater sustainability. Today, Madeira is noted for its unique winemaking process which involves heating the wine up to temperatures as high as 60°C (140°F) for an extended period of time in stoves or heating areas called " an Estufa" this method introduces some levels of oxidation. Due to this unique process, Madeira is a very robust wine that can be quite long lived even after being opened.

➢ **Marsala** is a wine produced in the region surrounding the Italian city of Marsala in Sicily. Marsala received Denominazione di origine controllata, or DOC, status in 1969.
  ▪ The wine is fortified much like Port. Like port, Marsala wine was fortified with brandy to ensure that it would last long ocean voyages, basically from port of call to ports of call. That style became traditional. Marsala at one time was quite popular and maintained an interest with other fortified wines such as Port and Sherry. Of late, Marsala has lost that level and is now relegated more to cooking than as an after dinner drink.
  ▪ Marsala is produced using the Grillo, Inzolia, and Catarratto white grape varietals, and a few others.

➢ **Sweet wines**

> *Commit to Memory*

  ▪ There are basically 3 means of producing sweet wines. Sweet wines are produced by the development of sugar (Brix) as the fruit develops on the vine or by controlling the ratio of sugar to water residing in the grape berry.
  • **Late Harvest Brix** (25 -30+)
    ◆ **Late harvest** is a term used for wines made from grapes left on the vine longer than usual. *Late harvest* is usually an indication of a sweet dessert wine, such as late harvest Riesling. Late harvest grapes are often more similar to raisins, but have been naturally dehydrated while on the vine.
  • **Botrytis Cinerea (Noble Rot)** Botrytis Brix (35+) approx.
    ◆ **Botrytis Cinerea** is a fungus that affects wine grapes. In viticulture, it is commonly known as botrytis bunch rot. The fungus comes in two different kinds of infections on grapes. The first is grey rot, a result of consistently wet or humid conditions. This is not desirable and results in the loss of the affected bunch. <u>The second, noble rot</u>, occurs when drier conditions follow wetter, and can result in distinctive sweet dessert wines, such as Sauternes or the Aszú of Tokaj. The species name Botrytis cinerea is derived from the Latin for "grapes like ashes", this refers to the bunching of the fungal spores on their conidiophores, and "ashes" just refers to the grey like color of the spores.
  • **Eiswein (Ice Wine)**
    ◆ **Ice wine** or in Germany, **Eiswein** is a type of dessert wine produced from grapes that have been partially frozen while still on the vine. The sugars and other

dissolved solids do not freeze, but the water does, allowing a more concentrated grape must to be pressed from the frozen grapes, resulting in a smaller amount of more concentrated, very sweet wine. A rough visual of this can be recalled from enjoying a popcycle and sucking the flavored juice out while leaving a frozen stick of ice. Ice wine grapes should not be made from affected by Botrytis Cinerea or noble rot, at least not to any great degree. This gives ice wine a unique refreshing sweetness balanced by high acidity. Due to the intense labor effort and risky production process the result is a fairly small yield, making it generally quite expensive.

- **MLF Malolactic Fermentation**
  - This is the conversion of malic acid that resides in wine to lactic acid and carbon dioxide by use of lactic bacteria.
  - One of the key reasons' for using the process is to soften the wine from the harsher malic acid, rounding off the rougher edges to a smoother Lactic acid.
- Malic Acid => Latic Acid
  - **Malic acid** is one of several organic acids present in grapes.
  - **Lactic acid** is a weak organic acid that is produced by lactic acid bacteria from malic acid.
  - Bacteria / pH 3 -4
    - Power of the Hydrogen ion
    - pH effects taste, color, longevity and microbiology stability.
- **Fruit Acid**: naturally occur in grape / berry juice.
  - **Tartaric** (principal organic acid of most vinifera grapes)
    - Without wine is insipid
  - **Malic**
    - Geared for white wines
  - **Citric Acid**
    - Is the lesser naturally occurring acid in the grape juice.
    - Lowers pH and increases Titratable acidity

- Process
  - Fining
    - Egg whites, Bentonite (removes organics (protein haze)) from the wine. The fining material such as egg whites are beaten in a large container and then added to the wine in the vat. The egg white bonds with the suspended solids and settles to the bottle of the vat, where later the wine is racked off and the egg white contents are degraded.
    - Gelatins and other polyclear materials are used in the same fashion.
  - Filtering
    - A mechanical means of exacting larger solids suspended in the wine. The process in common to filtering water, or oil filter for you car. It is a typically a corrugated paper or synthetic fibrous material to catch solids moving through a pump inline with the filter system.

➢ Enjoying white wines (tasting)
  ▪ Temperature
    • Making white wines: the fermentation temperature is typically cooler than when making red wine. Most are controlled by use of doubled jacketed stainless steel tanks.
    • Most white wine is served at a lower temperature than red wine but typically warmer than Champagne or Sparkling wines for the most part.

➢ Tartaric Acid
  ▪ Tartaric Acid is a main acid in wines, that provide the liveliness in the wine, the others being Malic acid, Lactic acid, and Citrus acid. Tartaric acid becomes visible and obvious in a glass of wine that was not been "chill proof" a means of stabilizing the wine at colder temperatures. When wines that have not undergone this process and are stored in a refrigerator for some length of time and then severed the Tartaric acid will fall out of solution and crystallize at the bottom of the glass appearing as broken glass. Often the customer will ask to return the wine because of this, thinking there is broken glass in their wine. Swirling the wine in the glass at a warmer temperature will completely dissolved the Tartaric acid back into a solution.

➢ Enjoying red wines (tasting)
  ▪ Temperatures
    • Making red wines: the fermentation temperature is typically warmer than when making white wine. Red wines are still controlled by use of doubled jacketed stainless steel tanks most of the time, but are allowed to reach a higher temperatures for better extraction of color and intensity.
  ▪ Most red wines are served at a warmer temperature than white wine
  ▪ Oxidation
    • The process where grape juice or wine reacts with oxygen producing an undesirable odor and changes in flavor. Exceptions to this would be Sherry for instance.
  ▪ Sediment
    • Occurs by the fallout of solids suspended in the Must or Wine over some period of time. This can also become part of the Lees (dead or typically call spent yeast).
  ▪ Decanting
    • Decanting is a process used to separate the wine from the sediment. This is becomes necessary in older wines that have been stored for quite some time. Or the use of a decanter to allow the wine to breath (exposed to a much larger volume of air and air surface.

GRAPES OF FRANCE:
WILL BE COVERED IN EACH REGION

FRANCE: KEY REGIONS
DISCUSSED IN COUNTRY:

*BORDEAUX
*BURGUNDY
*ALSACE
*CHAMPAGNE
*LOIRE VALLEY
*RHONE VALLEY

QUALITY CONTROLS AND LAWS:
- Vin de Table (VdT)
- Vin de Pays (VdP)
- Vin Délimitè de Qualité Supérieure (VDQS)
- Appellation d' Origine Contrôlee (AOC)

The levels of quality control and countrywide laws for France

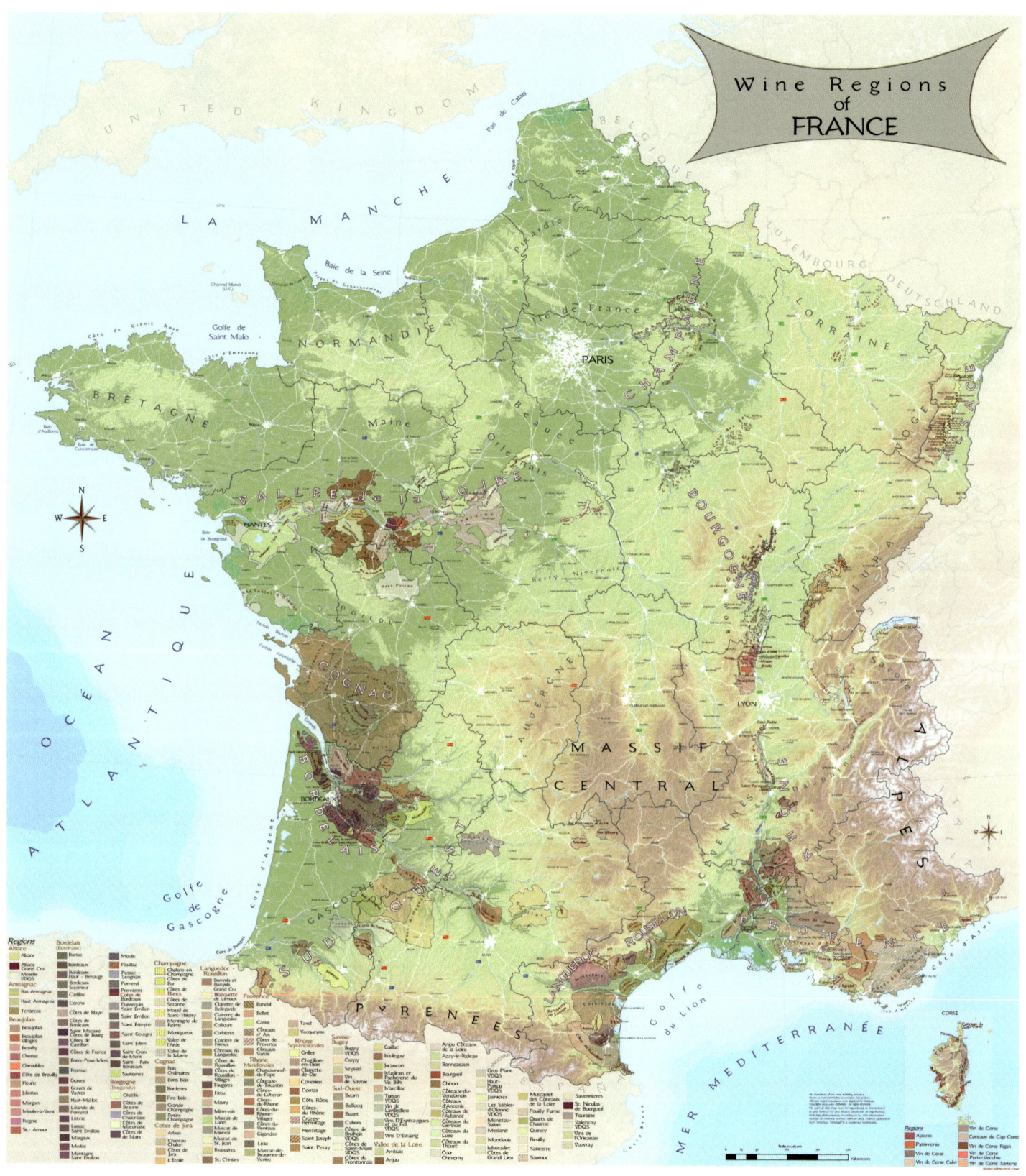

Chapter 3
France

Comments on France; the perception of the wines of France in respect to the rest of the world can be considered an ongoing challenge. Over the centuries many have thought France to be the Mecca of the wine world. The French have accepted this notion as recently as the time of the printing this book and not without merit, and why not. The majority of the most common internationally known noble varietals hale from France. In addition to this noble contribution of France, they made great strides and greater success, in establishing quality control laws that not only regulated but relegated the use of certain varietals to particular regions within France. Their 1855 classification is a prime example of this. The French are very passionate about their food and even more so about their wines. It can be stated that the French held title to this recognition without challenge as the rest of the world looked on with acceptance. Through the centuries, prominent individuals have documented the outstanding wines of France. Thomas Jefferson for instance, in his many trips to France paid considerable recognition to places like Bordeaux and Chateau Haut Brion. France's strong strategy was "food and wine" pairing, early on attention to the marriage of wine to French cuisine and the establishment of the "Appellation d' Origine Contrôlee" (AOC) or AC. The use of the term Appellation is the key here. Other countries including the United States, inappropriately use the terms such as; Champagne, Burgundy and Chablis to name theirs wines as opposed to the recognized region that is protected and legally defined as a geographical area where grapes for wine were grown such as in France. Champagne, Burgundy and Chablis for instance are regions (legally recognized appellations in France not a varietal). Most European wine regions identify their wines by their appellation (Germany is one exception) versus new world which identify by the varietal and therefore to use such terms in the United States and other countries is an infringement on these well established and governed practices.

➢ Vin de Table (VdT)
 ▪ This is basic table wine. Grapes can be used from anywhere in France with no greater pedigree. There no restriction or specifications.
➢ Vin de Pays (VdP)
 ▪ This level moves up the chain of pedigree with just a few add on restrictions. Instead of anywhere within France, Vin de Pays falls into 3 basic types, regional, departmental and or

by zone. Either way, the breath is small than VdT but still covers a very large area, that will vary significantly of soils, viticulture behavior, micro-climate and a number of growers.

➢ Vin Délimitè de qualité supérieure (VDQS)

▪ This is a very small category, basically a holding place for those growers and or produces expecting to continue to improve in the near future to an AOC level. This represents less than 2% in this of wines with this status. The wines are produced under INAO guidelines and controls.

➢ Appellation d' Origine Contrôlee (AOC)

▪ This is the highest level of quality control. AOC wines have very specific requirements. The wines must comply with grapes approved for that appellation and made from 100% of the grapes allowed. The grapes would need to have been grown within the limits or area specified basically a smaller geographical area, minimum levels of sugar (Brix) during harvest and minimum levels alcohol after fermentation. The grapes would have maximum yields per (hectare about 2.2 acres). The wine making practice (methods for the region or appellation must conform to the INAO. The bottling must take place in the same and wines must pass the INAO taste test, more for meeting the expectation of the region's Terrior (see definition).

Regions of France covered with interest: (You should commit these regions to memory). These regions are responsible for less than 25% of all wines produced in France but represent the most famous and sought after wines in France.

The Six key areas of France you should know.

Bordeaux:
Burgundy:
Alsace:
Champagne:
Loire Valley:
Rhone Valley:

Other wine Regions not covered in this interest:

Southwest:	Sovoie and Jura	Corsica
Bergerac	Provence	Cognac
Midi	Lanuedoc – Rossillon	

GRAPES OF BORDEAUX:

RED	WHITE
CABERNET SAUVIGNON	SAUVIGNON BLANC
MERLOT	SEMILLON
CABERNET FRANC	MUSCADELLE
PETIT VERDOT	
MALBEC	

BORDEAUX: KEY COMMUNES DISCUSSED IN REGION:

*Medoc
*Saint- Estèphe
*Pauillac
*St-Julien
*Haut-Medoc
*Margaux
*Barsac
*Sauternes

Soil: Mostly gravel on the left Bank and a bit more Clay and limestone on the right Bank

Climate: Mild and moderated by Atlantic Ocean. A little cooler on the right Bank

QUALITY CONTROLS AND LAWS:

- Vin de Table (VdT)
- Vin de Pays (VdP)
- Vin Délimitè de Qualité Supérieure (VDQS)
- Appellation d' Origine Contrôlee (AOC)

The levels of quality control and countrywide laws for Bordeaux

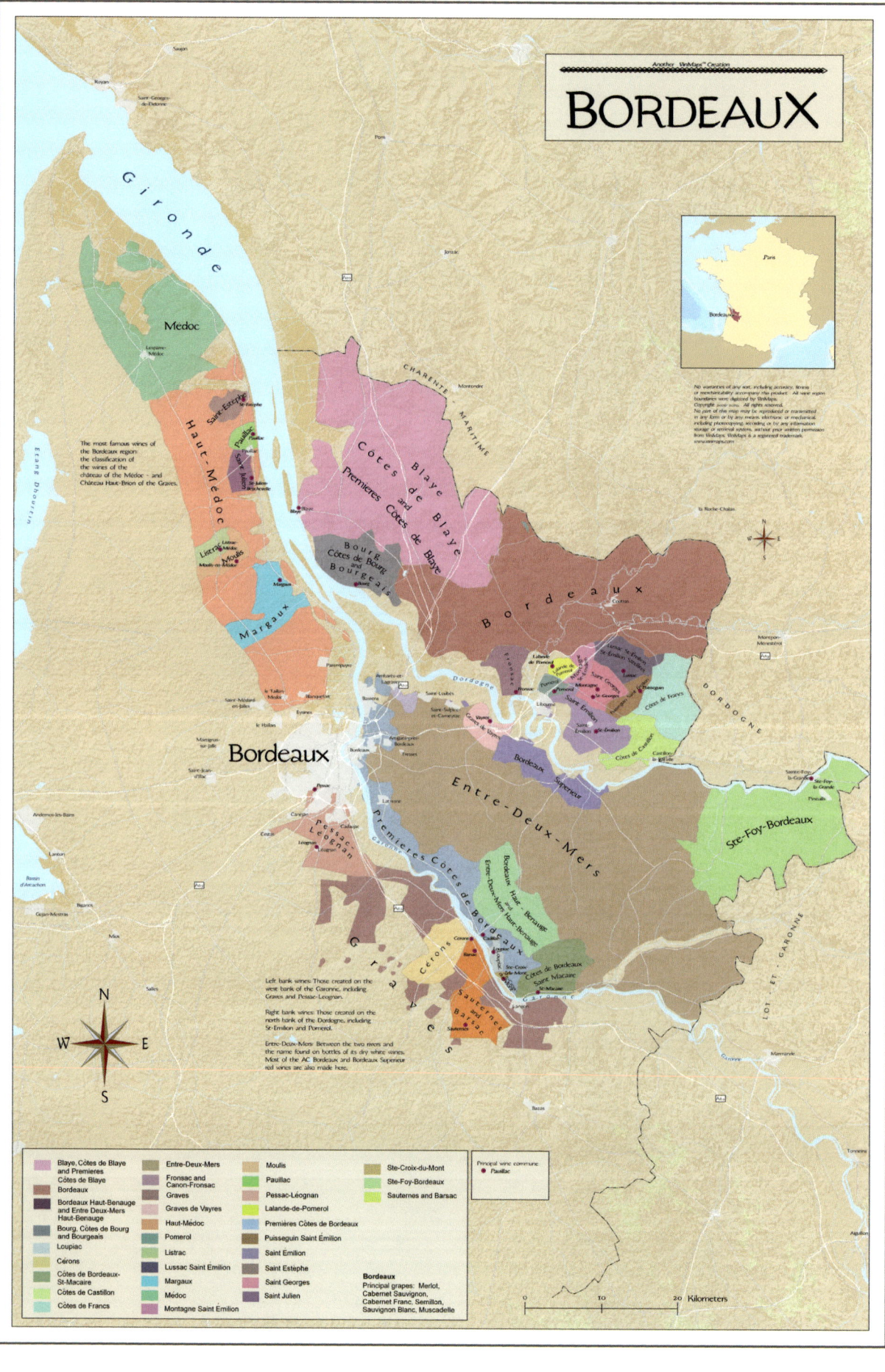

BORDEAUX

The most famous wines of the Bordeaux region: the classification of the wines of the château of the Médoc - and Château Haut-Brion of the Graves.

Left bank wines: Those created on the west bank of the Garonne, including Graves and Pessac-Léognan.

Right bank wines: Those created on the north bank of the Dordogne, including St-Emilion and Pomerol.

Entre-Deux-Mers: Between the two mers and the name found on bottles of its dry white wines. Most of the AC Bordeaux and Bordeaux Superieur red wines are also made here.

Blaye, Côtes de Blaye and Premieres	Entre-Deux-Mers	Moulis	Ste-Croix-du-Mont
Côtes de Blaye	Fronsac and Canon-Fronsac	Pauillac	Ste-Foy-Bordeaux
Bordeaux	Graves	Pessac-Léognan	Sauternes and Barsac
Bordeaux Haut-Benauge and Entre Deux-Mers Haut-Benauge	Graves de Vayres	Lalande-de-Pomerol	
Bourg, Côtes de Bourg and Bourgeais	Haut-Médoc	Premières Côtes de Bordeaux	Principal wine commune
Loupiac	Pomerol	Puisseguin Saint Émilion	Pauillac
Cérons	Listrac	Saint Emilion	
Côtes de Bordeaux-St-Macaire	Lussac Saint Émilion	Saint Estephe	
Côtes de Castillon	Margaux	Saint Georges	**Bordeaux**
Côtes de Francs	Médoc	Saint Julien	Principal grapes: Merlot, Cabernet Sauvignon, Cabernet Franc, Semillon, Sauvignon Blanc, Muscadelle
	Montagne Saint Emilion		

0   10   20   Kilometers

Bordeaux

History and Description

Bordeaux is one of the most recognize, respected and largest wine region's in the world. As mentioned earlier, when talking about European wines, we must continue to make note that their wines for the most part are identified by the region and not by the varietal; Alsace is the one exception. In this case, Bordeaux is a city, a wine region, and the name of the wine. Confusing? Yes it can be, especially for those who have started or brought up with new world wine thinking, making the Varietal the noted wine and not the region, understanding neither to be considered good or bad but just different.

Soil and Climate: THE TERRIOR

1855 classification:

- It is, probably common in human nature, to rank and rate any point of interest. Who is the best, who is the most expensive, who is the most sought after? Common and typically expected questions from anyone or group seeking to quantify and organize a ranking classification. Many would find this useful, when marketing, purchasing, collecting or simply categorizing something of interest. Bordeaux felt no differently about their wines. Napoleon III was one such individual that felt the need for this identification and had requested a sorting of the wines of the Medoc. Over the previous decades, there had been various rankings and discussions along such lines, any given collectors or merchants (négoçiants) had made their own set of who's who, by price, demand and visibility to the market but nothing so recognized and maintained as the 1855 classification of the Medoc. During this time, the Paris "World's Fair" was fast approaching and this type of ranking would proved to be most informative if formalized and available by that time. Napoleon's request was immediately taken on and addressed by the very same négoçiants that had been collecting their own personal data for sometime. Their criteria were collections of what wines had fetched the high prices, most sought after, most recognized (including the collecting behavior of Thomas Jefferson's affinity to Haut – Brion). The merchant, decided on breaking the ranking into 5 levels or growths (Cru). This ranking applies to the Medoc with few exceptions. Originally there were four 1st growth sites permitted from the 1855 classification. Mouton Rothschild (Pauillac) was actually placed in the 2nd growth category initially and it wasn't until much later 1976 that through an enormous amount of petitioning and negotiating was Mouton Rothschild (Pauillac) elevated to 1st growth. Now making a total of five 1st Chateaus'. Amazingly there has not been another elevated Chateau or change in status since that time.

1st growth or Premier cru
2nd growth or Deuxieme
3rd growth or Troisièmes
4th growth or Quatrièmes
5th growth or Cinquièmes

1ˢᵗ Growth

- Latour (Pauillac)
- Mouton Rothschild (Pauillac)
- Lafite Rothschild (Pauillac)
- Haut-Brion
- Margaux (Margaux)

Commit to Memory

Bordeaux and its Communes:

Medoc
    St Estèphe
    Pauillac
    St- Julien

Haut-Medoc
    Listrac
    Moulis
    Margaux

Note: Chateau is often abbreviated as => Ch.

Many will clearly admit, there is a certain mythical, mystical, and magical fascination with one of the most powerful wine region in the world and a good part of this is attributed to the feeling that even with a lifetime's study, there will always be something new to discover about Bordeaux. I would hold this to be very true about most wine regions in general but Bordeaux is most captivating.

Bordeaux is France's largest quality wine region. Wine has been produced in Bordeaux for 2,000 years. Individual districts reflect a certain uniqueness and highly distinct personalities that are reflected in the wine they produce. The French like to call this "Terroir". This is a term the French use to completely reflect the totality of all growing essentials to wine, the soil and climate conditions for that region, the seasonal variations, the geological history, and this goes on. The bottom line to the term "Terrior" is everything and anything that relates to making that wine unique to that particular region. There are 57 different areas, or appellations, in Bordeaux. Recently, "Premières Côtes de Bordeaux, Côtes de Blaye, Côtes de Castillon, Côtes de Francs" are joining together to form one Côtes de Bordeaux region, so now 54.

In the spirit on this text the 54 has been reduced to what regions are most known and active within wine discussions and exams.

THE MÉDOC and HAUT-MÉDOC (Left Bank)

The left Bank is driven by Cabernet Sauvignon primarily but as mentioned, there are four other red varietals that may be blended in as Bordeaux.

The Médoc and Haut- Médoc is the most famous region in the Bordeaux. Starting with the city of Bordeaux and stretching northward for 50 miles along the left bank of the Gironde River. The northern 1/3 portion is the Medoc and the southern 2/3 part is the Haut- Medoc.

Margaux:

The southern most and largest commune of the Médoc is Margaux. It has more classified estates than St. Estephe, Pauillac, or St. Julien. Chateau Margaux itself is the major focus as well as 20 other well known properties.

Soil: light and gravelly.

Plump, silky and seductive are the words often used to describe wines from Margaux. Because of their style, they tend to be very friendly and more approachable when young. This is in part due to its "terroir" which is comprised of the thinnest soil as well as the highest proportion of rock size gravel in all of the Médoc. It drains well but also more susceptible to vintage variation. The wines tend to have the highest proportions of Merlot within the "core" of the Médoc further adding to its ample roundness and openness. It is home to the largest number of classified growths including its namesake first growth, Château Margaux.

St. –Julien:

Just north of the largest commune Margaux is the smallest, St. Julien. St. Julien has the highest percentage of classified growths about 95 percent of the wines are Second, Third or Fourth Growths, although there are no first or fifth growths.

St Julien falls in the middle of the Médoc as far as its character of wine style – not quite as assertive or aggressive as Pauillac or as seductive or alluring as Margaux. It falls strongly between the two more characterized communes and as a result, it's a product of both. Its wines have often been sought out by aficionados world wide. Despite the fact that it has no first growths, it has several second growths including Léoville Las Cases, Léoville Barton, Léoville Poyferré and Ducru Beaucaillou as well as the celebrated châteaux such as Talbot and Beychevelle.

Pauillac:

Three of the five First Growths are home in this soil. Ch. Lafite- Rothchild, Ch. Mouton-Rothchild, and Ch. Latour. What makes Pauillac so popular is that it has 18 of the 61 classified wines and the best of many. This region is considered king of the Left Bank communes. Its renowned well-draining, gravelly soils enable its dominant grape Cabernet Sauvignon to reach extreme levels of complexity and concentration. As a result, the wines tend to be full-bodied with full tannins and good freshness. The aromatic intensity of Pauillac wines are considered classic Bordeaux, pencil shavings and black currant with hints mint occasionally. Some of the most famous châteaux of the commune are Latour, Mouton Rothschild, Lafite Rothschild, Pichon Baron, Pichon Lalande and Lynch Bages.

St. –Estèphe:

This is the Medoc most northernmost commune. Know for a more rugged style of wines. Here the Chateaus have more Merlot and are closer to the mouth of Gironde River. The soil is made up of layers of gravel on top of a clay base, this is great for Merlot, the most planted variety in Bordeaux. Like St Julien, it is one of the four most important communal appellations of the Médoc which does not contain any first growths, despite its southern border from Château Lafite. Nonetheless, it is home to some outstanding châteaux such as the leading estate of Cos d' Estrournel, Montrose, Calon Segur and Lafon Rochet.

Graves /Pessac Léognan

Named for its gravelly soil, Graves is just south of the city of Bordeaux. Besides being well draining, it also adds profound mineral complexity to its wines and the only part of Bordeaux where both red and white wines are made by most Chateaus. The vineyards, were the first to be known internationally. Casks of wine were shipped to England as early as the 12th century and by the 16th several important estates were already established, including Graves most famous Ch. Haut-Brion. Haut-Brion was collected by the likes of Thomas Jefferson. Thomas Jefferson wrote about Haut-brion" and purchased large amounts and had it sent back to the states. Ch. Haut-Brion was the only property outside of Medoc and Sauturnes to be included in the 1855 classification. Haut-Brion has an almost primordial earthy character along with the sub-appellation Pessac-Lèognan. Many of the best red and white come from this area of ten tiny communes, grouped together by the French government in 1987. La Mission Haut Brion, Laville Haut Brion, Haut Bailly and Domaine de Chevalier.

Sauternes and Barsac:

Quite a bit south of Graves along the Garonne River (the Garonne and Dordogne are tributaries to the Gironde) are Bordeaux's sweet-wine-producing communes, the most important of which are Sauternes and Barsac, made mostly from Semillon and some Sauvignon Blanc.

The Right Bank or on the other side of the Medoc

Where the wines of the Left Bank are largely Cabernet Sauvignon, the Right Bank is Merlot dominate. The soil is more clay and limestone and a bit cooler for Merlot and some Cabernet Franc. And where the Médoc contains many large vineyards, the Right Bank is made up of a lot of smaller, vineyards.

- **Pomerol**
  - This is the smallest of the appellation, and was not part of the 1855 classification. It is exclusively red wines, actually ;(only 10% of white wine is produced in Bordeaux). Le Pin and Pétrus, are the big names in this region. Pomerol wines are among the most silky, luxurious and seductive wines in Bordeaux.
    - In (1979 produced the first vintage of 100% Merlot). This is what makes Pomerol … Pomerol!
    - The soils are predominately iron-rich clay with a bit of gravel mixed in to produce wines with extraordinary power and depth.
- **St. –Emilion:**

- Saint Emilion has two appellations; Saint Emilion and Saint Emilion Grand Cru.
- St Emilion. Similar to the Médoc, there is a classification system in place which dates from 1955 and outlines several levels of quality. These include its regional appellation of St Emilion, St Emilion Grand Cru, St Emilion Grand Cru Classé and St Emilion Premier Grand Cru Classé, to ensure better accuracy, the classification is redone every 10 years enabling certain chateaux's to be upgraded or downgraded depending on the quality of their more recent vintages.

Others regions not covered:

- Listrac and Moulis*
- Entre-Deux Mers
- Fronsac and Canon-Fronsac
- The Cotes
  - De blaye
  - De Bourg

GRAPES OF BURGUNDY:

RED	WHITE
<u>RED</u>	<u>WHITE</u>
PINOT NOIR	CHARDONNAY
GRAPE OF BEAUJOLAIS	
GAMAY	

BURGUNDY: KEY APPELLATIONS DISCUSSED IN REGION:

*Chablis
*Cote d'Or
   *Côte de Nuits
   *Côte de Beaune
* Côte Chalonnaise
*Mâconnais
*Beaujolais Crus
*Beaujolais

SOIL: Limestone; some Chalk

Climate: moderate to Continental

QUALITY CONTROLS AND LAWS:

- Bourgogne (this is standard table wine)
- Village
- Premier Cru
- Grand Cru

The Appellation Controllée Laws provide four different levels for Burgundy

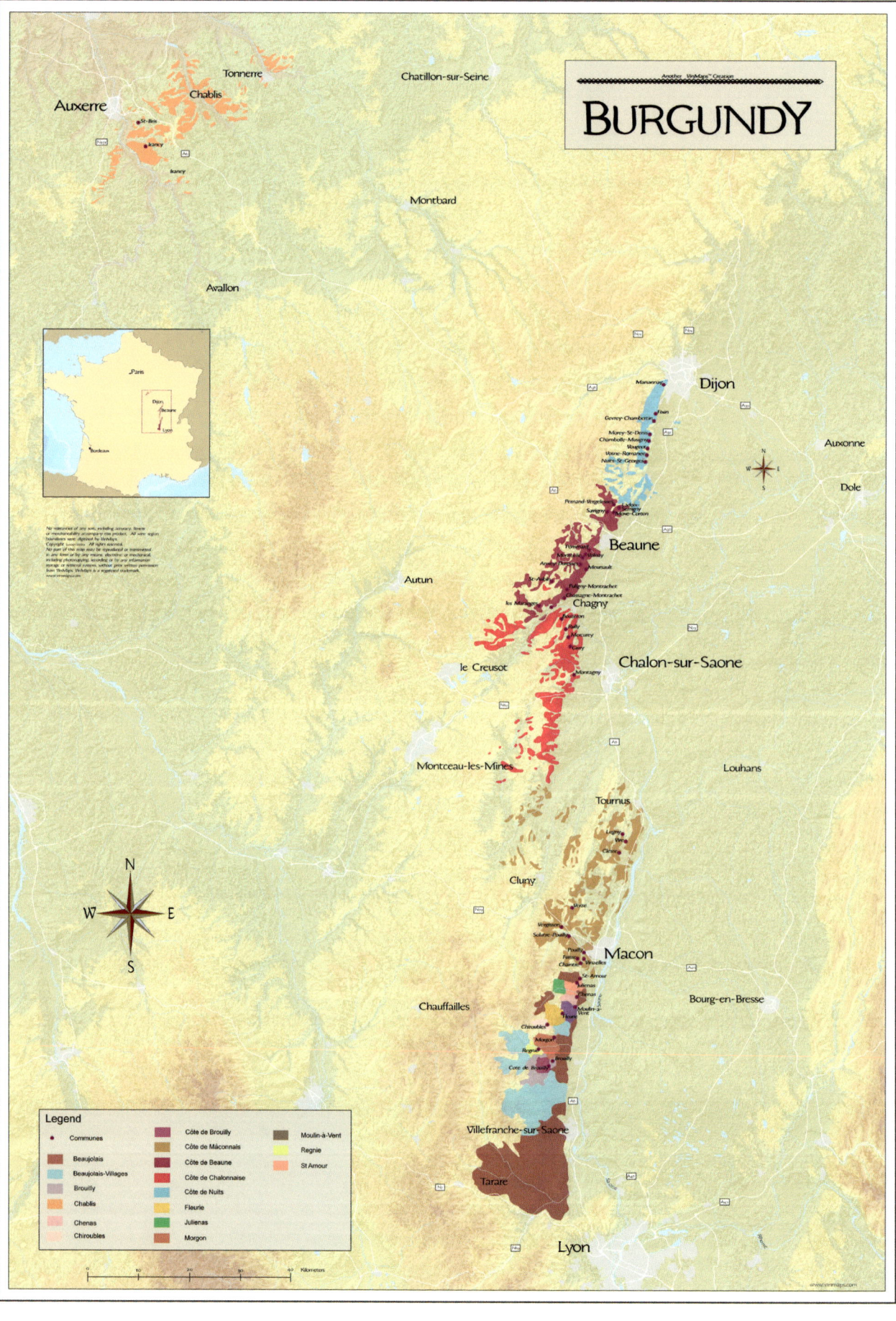

BURGUNDY

Another VinMaps™ Creation

Tonnerre

Chatillon-sur-Seine

Auxerre

Chablis

St-Bris

Irancy

Irancy

Montbard

Avallon

Paris

Dijon
Beaune
Lyon

Bordeaux

Marsannay

Dijon

Gevrey-Chambertin

Fixin

Auxonne

Morey-St-Denis
Chambolle-Musigny
Vougeot
Vosne-Romanée
Nuits-St-Georges

Dole

Pernand-Vergelesses
Savigny
Aloxe-Corton
Pommard

Beaune

Autun

Volnay
Meursault

St-Aubin

Puligny-Montrachet

les Maranges

Chassagne-Montrachet

Chagny

Chalon-sur-Saone

Rully
Mercurey
Givry

le Creusot

Montagny

Montceau-les-Mines

Louhans

Tournus

Lugny
Viré
Clessé

Cluny

Viré

Viré

Mâcon

Vinzelles
Solutré-Pouilly
Pouilly
Fuissé
Chaintré Vinzelles

Bourg-en-Bresse

St-Amour
Juliénas
Chénas
Moulin-à-Vent

Chauffailles

Chiroubles

Morgon

Régnié

Brouilly

Côte de Brouilly

Villefranche-sur-Saone

Tarare

Lyon

Legend

• Communes	▪ Côte de Brouilly	▪ Moulin-à-Vent
▪ Beaujolais	▪ Côte de Mâconnais	▪ Regnie
▪ Beaujolais-Villages	▪ Côte de Beaune	▪ St Amour
▪ Brouilly	▪ Côte de Chalonnaise	
▪ Chablis	▪ Côte de Nuits	
▪ Chenas	▪ Fleurie	
▪ Chiroubles	▪ Julienas	
	▪ Morgon	

Kilometers

0   10   20   30   40

www.vinmaps.com

Burgundy:

➤ Well this is where things get really interesting. Burgundy is certainly considered complicated if not out right difficult. One of the key areas of complexity is the fact that there are so many landowners taking part in such a small wine growing arena. There are 4 départements of Burgundy; the Cote d'Or, Yonne, Nievre, and the Saone-et-Loire. The heart of Burgundy is approximately 25 miles long and just around a mile wide. In addition, there are more than 2,045 Communes (keep in mind, this is all Pinot Noir or Chardonnay but the wines will reflect the name of the commune, you can now appreciate the range of understanding the layout of Burgundy.

➤ **Burgundy is known for some of the most expensive and famous wines in the world.**

➤ Burgundy experiences an interesting type of continental climate with very unpredictable rains and frost and this may completely occur during harvest time. Because of this climate, there is a lot of variation between vintages. Which makes Burgundy wines so fascinating and worthy of tracking by vintage.

➤ "Grand Cru" vineyards are usually grown from the middle and higher part of the slopes, most exposure to sunshine and the best drainage, the "Premier Cru" is grown from the middle to the lower slopes. The "Village" wines are typically produced on flatter terrain nearer the villages. The Bourgogne quality level again mimics the general table wine. Grapes can come from anywhere in Burgundy, without much status.

➤ The Côte de Nuits has 24 out of the 25 red Grand Cru appellations in Burgundy, while Côte de Beaune has all of the white Grand Crus with one exception.
  - Regions (the wine takes on the name of the region)
  - Basic quality controls levels
    - Bourgogne
    - Village
    - Premier Cru
    - Grand Cru

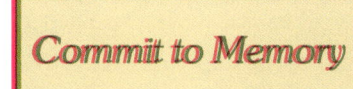

The following are the key regions within Burgundy; starting from the most northern area of Burgundy and proceeding south from there.

➤ **Chablis**
  - Soil conditions mostly (Limestone). This is Chardonnay of the most northern sub-region of Burgundy. Frost in the spring can present a major problem. There is some distance between Chablis and the start of the Cote d'Or.

➤ **Cote d'or**
  - 30 miles long escarpment; which is divided into two sections. The most northern of the Cote d' Or is the Côte de Nuits covering 1/3 and the Côte de Beaune covering the remaining 2/3's
    - **Côte de Nuits**
      - Northern part is responsible for most of the (top reds) and of course meaning Pinot Noir

- **Cote de Beaune**
  - Southern part and produces both (reds and whites); Pinot Noir and Chardonnay.
- ➢ **Cote Chalonnaise**
  - Further south is the Côte Chalonnaise, where again a mix of mostly red and white wines are produced
  - The other areas are; Mercurey, Rully and Givry and are less well known than their counterparts in the Côte d'Or.
- ➢ **Mâconnais**
  - Moving further south is Mâconnais with Pouilly-Fuisse as a well known and often popular Chardonnay.
- ➢ **Beaujolais:** Located in the most southern part of Burgundy and about 35 miles long and 9 miles wide. Beaujolais is considered to be in the southern part of Burgundy but actually falls under the Rhone départment.
  - **Quality (categories)**
    - Beaujolais
    - Beaujolais Villages
    - Beaujolais Cru

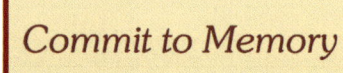

Commit to Memory

  - Soil conditions mostly decomposed granite, some sedimentary rock, clay and a little limestone.
  - Cru areas are mostly on Granite hills …elevation about 1,000 ft.
  - Gamay (noir)
  - Chardonnay and Aligote'
    - (California Gamay Beaujolais is not related whatsoever to French Gamay or Beaujolais) it is a clone of Pinot Noir and strictly used in California. There is also a Napa Gamay which is a French grape called **Valdiguie'**. Of course the French would like the name Beaujolais completely dropped and not used.
- ➢ **Carbonic Maceration (use rather extensively in Beaujolais)**
  - This is a process where whole berries (uncrushed) are introduced to the vat as opposed to crushing the berries before inoculation. Air is removed by pumping in "Carbon Dioxide". Doing this causes fermentation to actually take place inside the berry, this process, minimizes, alcohol, malic acid and allows the fruiter aromatic characteristics of the grape. The grapes are later pressing and the juice available. This wine is the made for immediate consumption, (great for the harvest celebratory practice in Burgundy as the harvest of the Pinot Noir and Chardonnay comes in for the season). The festival type Burgundy celebration as now been adopted by the States and not uncommon to see Beaujolais party events taking place in North America.
- ➢ **Beaujolais Nouveau**
  - Also called Vin Premier (first wine)
  - The 3rd Thursday in November.
- ➢ **Sparkling wines of Burgundy are:**
  - Known as Crèmant de Bourgogne. This is done with at least 30% Chardonnay and / or Pinot Noir and can have the addition of other grapes such as Aligoté. The wine is made by the same process as Champagne but again keep in mind not called Champagne due to the recognized region and associated method of Champagne.

GRAPES OF ALSACE:

WHITE	RED
*PINOT BLANC	*PINOT NOIR
RIESLING	
*SYLVANER	
PINOT GRIS	
*CHASSELAS	
* CHARDONNAY	
MUSCAT	

*not a noble grape

SOIL: Fertile alluvial, Granite, Limestone, Schist, Clay, Marl, Sandstone, Slate

Climate: Semi-continental

QUALITY CONTROLS AND LAWS:
- Regular, Reserve, and Late Harvest
- Bottle must be in a flute style
- Vendange Tardive
- Selection de Grains Nobles
- Grand Cru (about 50 plus vineyards)

The Appellation Controllée Laws provide regulations and levels for Alsace. Listed above Notably

Alsace

Alsace is approximately 300 miles east of Paris and falls in the most North – Eastern region of France between the Vosges Mountains in the west the Rhine River in the east, adjacent to Germany. Alsace has a great deal of German influence and becomes the one exception when it comes to the label of Alsace Wines. The wines are actually identified by the varietal unlike the rest of France identifying the wines by the regions. The region of Alsace consists of two departments, Bas-Rhin and Haut-Rhin Climate: Semi-continental climate with cold and dry winters and hot summers

➢ Grand Cru wines of Alsace as of
  ▪ 1983 received superior recognition of vineyard sites
    • Initially 25 were identified with a later additional of 25 more and this number is increasing.
    • There are 4 noble grape varietals that can be used by **Grand Cru Vineyards for their wines.**
      ◆ Riesling
      ◆ Gewürztraminer
      ◆ Pinot Gris
      ◆ Muscat

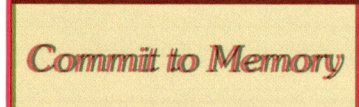

➢ Sparkling wines are made in Alsace as well using the same method as the region of Champagne but with the same exception of note: Not in the region of Champagne and therefore not allowed to call their Sparkling wines Champagne. The sparkling wine of Alsace as in Burgundy is called: **Crémant d' Alsace** as with Burgundy, **Crémant d' Buorgogne.** Other varietals are grown and produced in Alsace listed are the following.
  ▪ Varietals (Non Grand Cru)
    • Pinot Blanc
    • Sylvaner
      ◆ Pinot Noir
      ◆ Chasselas

Sweet Wines of Alsace

➢ Styles of wine making within Alsace
  ▪ **Vendange Tardive**: is a sweet wine style noted in Alsace (Vendange => means harvest) Tardive => meaning late; therefore Late Harvest and is restricted to Alsace. These wines are made without the aid of Chaptalization and can vary from bone dry to very sweet. There is no regulation and means of determine the level of sweetness as it varies from wine producer to wine producer.
  ▪ **Selection de Grains Nobles**: This is a Botrytis style wine. Affected by Noble Rot and produces some of Alsace best and riches sweet wines.

- Most wines are Chaptalized with the exception of Vendange Tardive which require total natural sugars nor is acidification (adding acid to the existing <u>must</u>) practiced and Selection de Grains Nobles. Chaptalization is the addition a sugar (typically <u>cane sugar</u> or <u>beet sugar</u>).

Commit to Memory

GRAPES OF CHAMPAGNE:

RED	WHITE
PINOT NOIR	CHARDONNAY
PINOT MEUNIER	

CHAMPAGNE: KEY APPELLATIONS DISCUSSED IN REGION:

* The Montagne de Reims
* Vallee de la Marne
* Epernay

SOIL: Chalk

Climate: Cool to very cold

QUALITY CONTROLS AND LAWS:
- Non Vintage (NV)
- Vintage
- Prestige Cuvee
- Rosé
- Blanc de Noirs
- Blanc de Blancs

The Appellation Controllée Laws apply
Listed are styles for Champagne

Champagne

The Champagne region of France is less than 100 miles east of Paris

- ➢ Dom Pérignon
    - ▪ Is probably one of the most popular and well known names in the champagne world today! It has been popularized by a great effort in marketing and has been synonymous with any given celebration as with the name champagne itself. It is named after Dom Pérignon, a Benedictine monk who was an important quality pioneer for the Champagne wine effort but contrary to popular myths, did not discover the champagne method for making sparkling wines. What he is credited for is his ability to blend wines together consistently year after year bringing the present day name to the standard and recognition it now receives. Champagne legally can use 3 varietals of any combination of percentage; of Chardonnay, Pinot Noir and Pinot Meunier. Dom Pérignon's ability taste and blend is his claim to fame. History, indication ironically, that he was not necessary a wine drinker.

- ➢ **Styles based on sweetness (are recognized and used throughout the Champagne and Sparkling wine industry by most countries).**

    - ▪ **You should commit the order from dry to sweet to memory**
        - • **Extra Brut** 0 to .6% sugar
        - • **Brut** less than 1.5 % sugar
        - • **Extra Dry** 1.2 to 2% sugar
        - • **Sec** 1.7 to 3.5% sugar
        - • **Demi-Sec** 3.3 to 5% sugar
        - • **Doux** more than 5%

> *Commit to Memory*

    - ▪ A bit of trivia: How many bubbles are in a bottle of Champagne?… The answer 56 million. This comes from a study conducted by Bollinger Champagne company.

- ➢ The Region of **Champagne France**
    - ▪ Holds the title of "Champagne" this word has become synonymous with all sparkling wines. The name Champagne is relegated "Only" to the region of Champagne. Up until the last decade or so, many sparkling wine producers allowed the term champagne on their bottle. Champagne is a region is France and with respect to France, the name should not be used by others. As this has come about over the years, most countries and regions have selected other names for their sparkling wines. Outside of the Champagne region, other varietals are allowed and that sparkling wine is referred to as "Crémant and at least 30% of chardonnay and / or Pinot Noir should be used to maintain this style. Other varietals such as Aligoté are used.
        - • Blends are most common and should not be considered as an inferior wine on the contrary these are some of the best wines. Blends consist of a large number of still wines and came be over a number of previous years.

- Soil: (Terroir) plays a major role in this process. Champagne noted for great acid in the wine and its unique character can be attributed to:
  - Chalk
- Bottle type and size (is unique to Champagne or Sparkling wine). The way the carbon dioxide is produced in the wine is by the same method as mentioned in the earlier section; "how is it made" process. Under a closed environment, the CO_2 has no place to go and therefore under pressure it retreats into a liquid state and then only released into its gaseous form, when the wine opened. The pressure in measured in psi (Pounds per square inches or atmospheres, 15 psi per atmosphere. A bottle of sparkling wine may approach 4 atmospheres or close to 60 psi. This becomes a lethal projectile if not controlled properly when opening the bottle. Due to the significant pressure build up, the bottle must be capable of sustaining such pressure. The bottle for Sparkling wine therefore has a thicker glass wall than the normal 750ml bottle and the punt is the reinforcement for the bottom with a heavy cork and wire cage to support the prevention of forcing the cork off. Prior to this attention, bottles resting in racks would literally explode in respect to the weakest location of the bottle.
  - Opening a bottle (one should take extreme caution)

Champagne Houses

- ❖ Dom Pérignon
- ❖ Louis Roederer
- ❖ Moët & Chandon
- ❖ Bollinger
- ❖ Taittinger
- ❖ Piper Heidsieck
- ❖ Nicolas Feuillatte
- ❖ Deutz
- ❖ Mumm
- ❖ Veuve Clicquot
- ❖ Perrier-Jouët
- ❖ Charles Heidsieck
- ❖ Pommery
- ❖ Krug
- ❖ Laurent Perrier

Key regions of Champagne

- ➤ There are a number of regions within the Champagne. As stated in the process of keeping it to a manageable wine study level, the top 3 regions are noted below.
- ➤ **The Montagne de Reims**
  - ▪ Reims is a major player of Champagne and certainly the most prestigious. This region is primarily a red grape area. Pinot Noir and a bit of the lesser Pinot Meunier. If anything these two varietals add the backbone to any given blend. Their contribution is good acid

and bouquet (supplying the fruit in the nose). Keep in mind, blends are the key and Champagne Houses will use fruit from a number of sources to reach their overall goal.

➤ **The Vallee de la Marne**
- The Marne Valley, home of fruity, early ripening grape, Pinot Meunier, is the closest to Paris. South of the Montagne de Reims and west of Epernay, is the second region, the Vallee de la Marne, or the Marne Valley.
  - Moët, Perrier Jouët, Pol Roger are some of the key Champagne Houses.

➤ **Epernay**
- Approximately 15 miles south of Reims in the Marne department of the Champagne-Ardenne region, in the north of France.

GRAPES OF LOIRE VALLEY:
RED   WHITE
CABERNET FRANC   CHENIN BLANC
                 SAUVIGNON BLANC
                 MELON DE BOURGOGNE
(ONLY KEY GRAPES LISTED)

LOIRE VALLEY: KEY APPELLATIONS DISCUSSED IN REGION

Upper Loire:
   *Sancerre
   * Pouilly Fumé
Touraine
   *Vouvray
   *Chinon (red)
Anjou /Saumur
   *Savennières
   *Quarts de Chaume
Nantes
   Muscadet

SOIL: Chalky Limestone, Gravel

CLIMATE: From Continental to Maritime.

QUALITY CONTROLS AND LAWS:
- Vin de Table (VdT)
- Vin de Pays (VdP)
- Vin Délimitè de Qualité Supérieure (VDQS)
- Appellation d' Origine Contrôlee (AOC)

The Appellation Controllée Laws provide four different levels for Loire Valley

Loire Valley

➤ A very long region cutting across France, the Loire is a river that runs approximately 630 miles or so from the eastern part of the upper Loire across to the Atlantic Ocean. The Loire is divided into four main regions.
  ▪ The Upper – Loire
  ▪ Touraine
  ▪ Anjou-Saumur
  ▪ Muscadet
➤ Most of the Grapes Grown in the Loire Valley are as follows:

Grapes

Whites	Reds
▪ **Whites**	**Reds**
▪ **Arbois**	**Cabernet Franc**
▪ **Chardonnay**	**Cabernet Sauvignon**
▪ **Chenin blanc**	**Gamay**
▪ **Folle Blanche**	**Grolleau**
▪ **Melon de Bourgogne**	**Pinot Noir**
▪ **Sauvignon Blanc**	

❖ <u>**Loire Valley**</u>
  ➤ **Nantes**
    ▪ Known for one wine Muscadet made from Melon de Bourgogne, often just Melon. This area is in the most western part of the Loire and borders the Atlantic coast. Seafood and Muscadet are the combination to fame. The key areas are listed below:
      • Muscadet de Coteaux de la Loire
      • Muscadet Cotes de Grandlieu
      • Muscadet de Severe-et-Maine
  ➤ **Anjou-Saumur**
    ▪ The middle of Loire, probably the most fascinating and least known part of the Loire Valley. Most are medium to fully sweet wines with the most prestigious being Quarts de Chaume.
      • **Quarts de Chaume**
        ◆ Botrytis Cinerea is responsible for the Chenin Blanc producing these incredibly rich, floral and elelegent fruit style wines.
        ◆ Sweet wines … Chenin blanc
      • **Savennières**
        ◆ Maybe the best dry Chenin blanc
      • **Rosés** made with Grolleau (groslot)
      • **Red wines** …mostly Cabernet Franc or Cabernet Sauvignon.
      • **Sparkling** …By Law 7 varietals are permitted; Chenin Blanc, Chardonnay, Cabernet Franc, Sauvignon blanc, Gamay, Pinot Noir, Pineaud'aunis and Grolleau.

- **Cre'mant de Loire** (White or Rose') but must be made in the same manner as the Champagne Method.
➢ **Touraine** (due east of Anjou-Saumur) the Chateau's were built in the 17th and 18th century. The famous red wine appellations are found here.
  - Chinon (Cabernet Franc)
    - Is known for some of the best red in the Loire Valley and is considered to be the softest and most elegant from the other regions.
  - Vouvray (Chenin Blanc)
    - Vouvray can be made from very dry to medium to very sweet and some into sparkling. Botrytis Cinerea again will be responsible for the better naturally sweet Vouvrays.
  - Sancerre (what Chenin blanc is to Vouvray of Loire, as Sauvignon blanc is to Sancerre. Chalky limestone is the soil type. Sancerre is synonymous with white wine (Sauvignon blanc) but there is also:
    - Red and Rosé Sancerre are made (and from Pinot Noir and some Gamay)
➢ **Upper Loire**
  - The other very popular region for Sauvignon blanc is Puilly-Fumé. The word fume means "smoke". In the states (California) the term is also used with (Fume Blanc) which is not another varietal but Sauvignon Blanc as well. In many cases you will find Sauvignon Blanc treated much like Chardonnay in California, undergoing a fair amount of oak.

Loire Wine Regions
  - **Bourgueil**
  - **Chinon**
  - **Cremant de Loire**
  - **Menetou-Salon**
  - **Muscadet**
  - **Pouilly-Fumé**
  - **Quarts de Chaume**
  - **Sancerre**
  - **Savennières**
  - **Vouvray**

■

GRAPES OF RHONE VALLEY:

RED	WHITE
SYRAH	GRENACHE BLANC
MOURVÈDRE	VIOGNIER
CINSAUT	MARSSANNE
GRENACHE	ROUSANNE
PICPOUL NOIR	PICPOUL
TERRET NOIR	PICARDAN
	BOURBOULENC

RHONE VALLEY: KEY APPELLATIONS DISCUSSED IN REGION:

*NORHTERN
  *Condrieu
  *Chateau Grillet
  *Cote Rotie
  *St-Joseph
  *Hermitage
  *Croze Hermitageg
  *Cornas
*SOUTHERN
  *Cotes-du Rhone
  *Gigondas
  *Beaumes-de Venise
  *Vacqueyras
  *Chateauneuf-du-Pape

SOIL: Granite and decomposed Granite

Climate: North: Continental

South: Mediterranean

QUALITY CONTROLS AND LAWS:
- Vin de Table (VdT)
- Vin de Pays (VdP)
- Vin Délimitè de Qualité Supérieure (VDQS)
- Appellation d' Origine Contrôlee (AOC)

The Appellation Controllée Laws provide four different levels for Rhone Valley

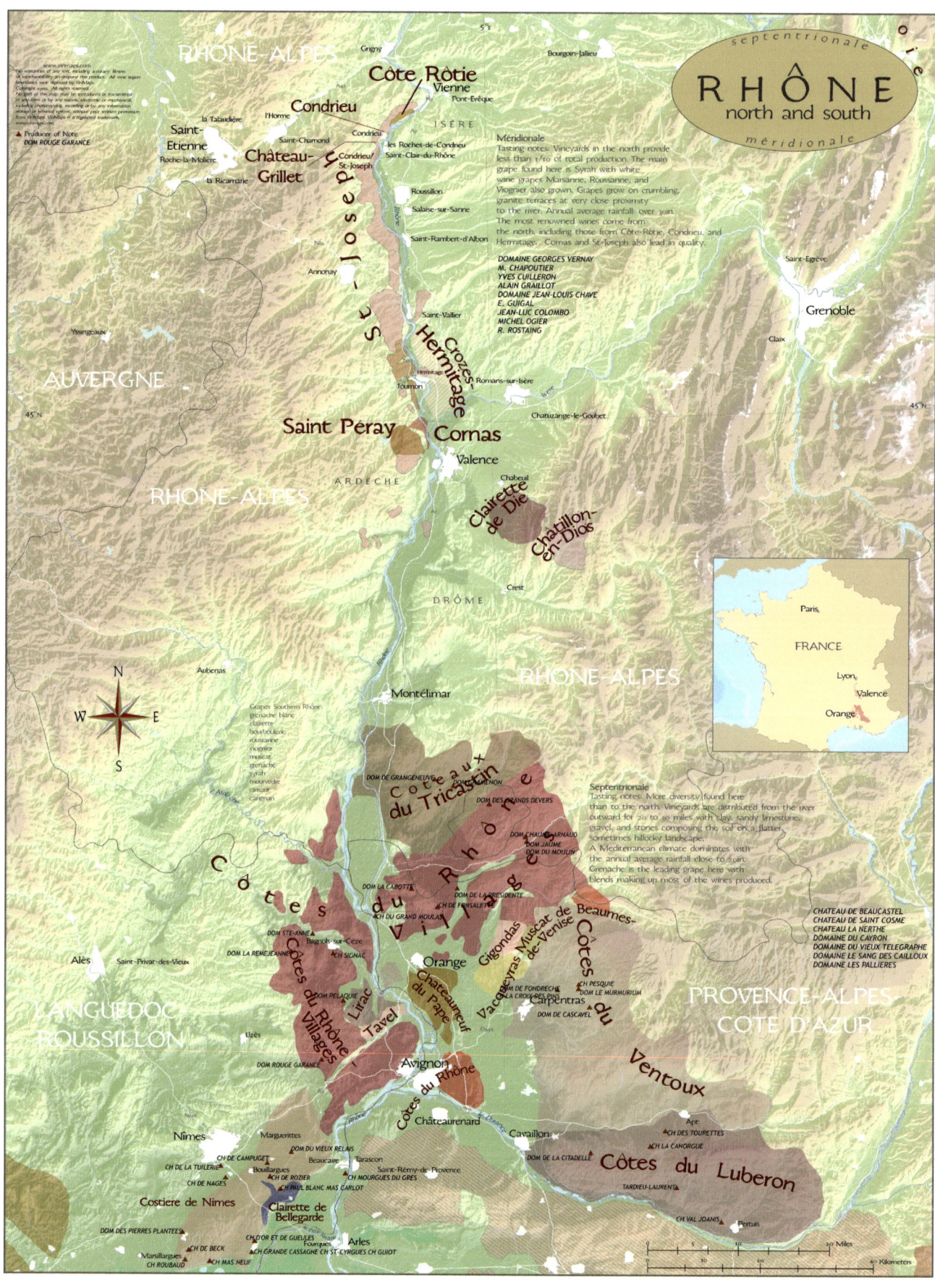

Rhone Valley:

Rhone Wines

<table>
<tr><td colspan="2"><u>Leading Appellations North</u></td></tr>
<tr><td>• Chateau Grillet</td><td>white</td></tr>
<tr><td>• Condrieu</td><td>white</td></tr>
<tr><td>• Cornas</td><td>red</td></tr>
<tr><td>• Cote – Rotie</td><td>red</td></tr>
<tr><td>• Crozes – Hermitage</td><td>red and white</td></tr>
<tr><td>• Hermitage</td><td>red and white</td></tr>
<tr><td>• St. Joseph</td><td>red and white</td></tr>
</table>

<table>
<tr><td colspan="2"><u>Leading Appellation South</u></td></tr>
<tr><td>• Beaumes - de – Venise</td><td>white fortified</td></tr>
<tr><td>• Chateauneuf – du – Pape</td><td>red and white</td></tr>
<tr><td>• Cotes –du – Rhone</td><td>red and white</td></tr>
<tr><td>• Cotes du Rhone-Village</td><td>red and white</td></tr>
<tr><td>• Gigondas</td><td>red and rose'</td></tr>
<tr><td>• Vacqueyras</td><td>red</td></tr>
</table>

The Rhone is named after the Rhone River and it is here that we depart from the more conventional sorting of the Grapes to regions and more formal view points to a more relaxed viewpoint and acceptance of blends. There are by most standards, twenty three different varietals that appear in the Rhone Valley, having said that, there are approximately 16 varietals that are considered important and worth committing most of those to memory.

❖ North (Appellations)

➢ **Cōte-Rôtie**
- Is the northernmost appellation. Producing some of the most expensive wines in the Rhone Valley. Cōte-Rôtie meaning "roasted hillside". This is all Syrah, no white wine produced in the region.
  - Syrah

- ➢ **Château-Grillet and Condrieu**
  - ▪ Château-Grillet and Condrieu Are the two major white wine areas for the northern region of the Rhone Valley, with Viognier as the key grape. This is the area where most of France's Viognier is grown. Luscious ripe fruit and exotic aromas of floral characteristics dominate this wine. These wines are typically expensive to very expensive

- ➢ **Condrieu**
  - ▪ Viognier

- ➢ **Château-Grillet**
  - ▪ Viognier

- ➢ **St. Joseph**
  - ▪ Syrah
  - ▪ Marsanne
  - ▪ Rousanne

- ➢ **Hermitage is the key area**
  - ▪ Here with the only red grape being Syrah. In addition there are 3 heavy used white varietal which are Viognier; Marsanne and Roussanne. This at one point in the wines of France was the most expensive, even to the likes of Bordeaux and Burgundy. This area sits on a 1,000ft Granite monolith. The red Hermitage is of course Syrah, white the white is a blend of Marsanne and Roussanne.
    - • **Key grapes**
      - ◆ Syrah (red)
      - ◆ Marsanne (white)
      - ◆ Roussanne (white)

- ➢ **Crozes-Hermitage**
  - ▪ Crozes-Hermitage for the most part, follows the path set by Hermitage, same grapes and close to the same style with this area producing a bit lighter and maybe softer style of wine.
    - • Syrah
    - • Marsanne
    - • Roussanne

- ➢ **Cornas** (Tiny area most south of the Northern Rhone region) Cornas, thought to have been derived from an old Celtic word for "burnt or scorched earth. Usually drunk after aging for 7 to 10 years
  - ▪ Syrah

> *Commit to Memory*

- **<u>Grape Varietals for the Rhone Valley</u>**

<u>RED</u>	<u>WHITE</u>
Grenache	Grenache blanc
Syrah	Clairette
Mourvedre	Bourboulenc
Cinsaut	Roussanne
Muscardin	Picpoul
Carignan	Picardan
Vaccarese	Muscat
Terret Noir	Marsanne

❖ **South (Appellations)** there is a significant gap between the northern Rhone and the Southern Rhone area. This area is much more of a Mediterranean climate whereas the northern region fit the continental version.

➢ **Gigondas** (The most northern of the Southern Rhone) Only red and rose' Gigondas are made. By law, the reds must be no more than 80% Grenache, with no less than 15% Syrah and / or Mourvedre blended in. The remaining fraction is often Cinsaut but may be made up of any other red Rhône grape except Carignan. All of Gigondas was once simply Côte-du-Rhône-Village. But in 1971 the reds and the rose's of the area were given a new, higher status and the appellation Gigondas, named after the nearby village, was born.
  - Grenache
  - Syrah
  - Mourvedre
  - Cinsaut

➢ **Vacqueyras** (appellation in 1990) is just south of Gigondas
  - Grenache
  - Syrah
  - Mourvedre
  - Cinsaut
  - Grenache Blanc
  - Clairette
  - Bourboulenc

➢ **Tavel**
  - Rose' (Bone dry and very robust are the typical style for this region)
    - Grenache (standard)
    - Others may be used in their rose'

➢ **Côtes-du-Rhône / Village**

- This is the area that produces the major of all wines from the Rhone Valley region. Approximately 75%.

	Red	White
•	Grenache	Grenache Blanc
•	Syrah	Clairette
•	Mourvedre	Bouroulenc
•	Cinsaut	Roussanne
•	Carignan	Viognier

➢ **Beaumes-de-Venise**
  - Vin doux naturel
    - Muscat / fortified wines
      - Specifically Muscat blanc à petits grains.

➢ **Chateauneuf-du-Pape**
  - The most celebrated southern region of the Southern Rhone wine is Chateauneuf du Pape. New Castle of the Pope… when in the fourteenth century the Pope resided in Avignon and NOT in Rome. As mentioned earlier, there are a large number of varietals that are permitted in the Rhone Region. The committed number to remember is thirteen or fourteen typically. Having said that, you will not find the chateaus utilizing more than a few of these varietals
  - Only Chateau Beaucastel grows and makes all with the full gamut.

There are a few other regions within the Rhone Valley that are not covered in this text.

GRAPES OF ITALY:
WILL BE COVERED IN EACH REGION

ITALY: KEY APPELLATIONS DISCUSSED IN REGION:

ITALY
NORTH – EASTERN
    *Fruili-Venezia Giulia
    *Veneto
    *Trentino-Alto Adige
NORTH – WESTERN
Piedmont
    *Barolo
    *Barberesco
    *Barbera d'Alba
    *Ghemme
    *Gattinara
    *Dolcetto
    *Brachetto d'Acqui
    *Asti
    *Cortese di Gavi
    *Moscatto d'Asti
CENTRAL
    Tuscany Tuscano
SOUTHERN
    *Campania
    *Basilicata
    *Sardinia
    *Puglia (Apulia)

QUALITY CONTROLS AND LAWS:

- Vino da Tavola (VdT)
- Indicazione Geografica Tipica (IGT)
- Donominazione di Origine Controllata (DOC)
- Donominazione di Origine
- Controllata Garantita(DOCG)

The Donominazione di Origine Controllata Laws provide four different levels for Italy

Italy

- ❖ In the discussion of Italy, we will cover the following regions: Once more I would like to stress that the regions covered are selected ones and there are regions intentionally omitted for the point of focus.
  - ▪ North-East Italy
  - ▪ North-West Italy
  - ▪ Central Italy
  - ▪ Southern Italy

- ❖ Quality Controls; Regulations and Laws
  - ➢ Basic ratings
    - ▪ Classification of Italy originally covered about 220 zones but new ones are being added regularly. The largest region in the Northwest part of Italy. It is the most important Italian region for quality wines.
      - • Vino da Tavola
      - • Indicazione Geografica Tipico (IGT)
        - ◆ Roughly equal the French Vin de pays.
        - ◆ Approx 120 areas under this control
      - • DOC approx 300 areas given this status
      - • DOCG approx 21 areas given this status
        - ◆ Permissible grape varieties
        - ◆ Maximum yield of grapes per hectare
        - ◆ Minimum degree of alcohol the wine must have
        - ◆ Pruning and trellising systems
        - ◆ Requirements for aging

GRAPES OF NORTH- EASTERN ITALY:

RED	WHITE
CABERNET FRANC	SAUVIGNON BLANC
MERLOT	PINOT GRIGIO
REFOSCO	PINOT BIANCO
CORVINA	GARGANEGA
RONDINELLA	TREBBIANO
MOLINARA	PROSECCO
SCHIAVA	MÜLLER THURGAU
TEROLDEGO	

ITALY: KEY
APPELLATIONS
DISCUSSED IN REGION:

NORTH-EASTERN
*Fruili-Venezia Giulia
   *Isonzo
   *Collio
   *Colli Orientali
*Veneto
   *Bardolino
   *Recioto di Soave
   *Valpolicella

*Trentino-Alto Adige
   *Alto Adige
   *Trentino

SOIL: Volcanic; Limestone; Gravelly Clay.

CLIMATE: Mediterranean

QUALITY CONTROLS AND LAWS:
- Vino da Tavola (VdT)
- Indicazione Geografica Tipica (IGT)
- Donominazione di Origine Controllata (DOC)
- Donominazione di Origine
- Controllata Garantita(DOCG)\

The Donominazione di Origine Controllata Laws provide
four different levels for North – Eastern Italy

North-East Italy

- ❖ Fruili-Venezia-Guilia
  - ➢ Friuli-Venezia Giulia (located in the Northeast bordering Slovenia and Austria)
    - ▪ There are ten DOC zones in Fruili-Venezia Guilia. The wines are both single varietals and in many cases blended whites. In the past much of the wines were made by the old traditional generations using large barrels and somewhat neutral oak. As new technology made its way in through the new generations and education, some of the best stainless steel wines are now available that are crisp, fruity with lively acids and zest .
    - ▪ One of the popular and key wines in this area is (was) Tocai Friulano is noted only due to a change of its name. As with many misused terms, Champagne, Burgundy, and Chablis, so was the use of Tocai. A Hungarian dessert wine in the region of Tocai, was used up to recently in the Northeastern part of Italy and now the name has been dropped respectfully as there is no region in Italy called Tocai.
    - ▪ **Whites** (the following list can produce some of the Super-Whites, any combination from the following)
      - • Chardonnay
      - • Picolit(a native grape from which an expensive and often overrate sweet wine is produced)
      - • Pinot bianco
      - • Ribolla Gialia
      - • Sauvignon Blanc
      - • Pinot Grigio
    - ▪ **Reds**
      - • Cabernet Franc
      - • Cabernet Sauvignon
      - • Merlot
      - • Refosco
      - • Schioppettino
      - • Tazzelenghe

- ❖ Trentino-Alto Adige
  - ➢ Trentino-Alto Adige Trentino covers about 20 different types of wine. (Alto Adige is largely German speaking Province and covers about 24 different types of wine)
    - ▪ Whites
      - • Chardonnay
      - • Müller Thurgau
      - • Nosiola
      - • Pinot Bianco
      - • Sauvignon Blanc
      - • Traminer

- Reds
  - Cabernet Franc
  - Cabernet Sauvignon
  - Logrein
  - Lambrusco
  - Marzemino
- ➤ Trentino (deep red wine, zesty and best drunk young)
  - Merlot
  - Schiava or Verntsch … also know as Trollinger in Württemberg Germany
    - Santa Maddalena
  - Teroldego

❖ The Veneto
  - ➤ There are two DOCG's in this region.
    - Recioto di Soave
    - Bardolino
      - Veneto ranks number three in the overall production for wine in Italy. There are twenty three DOC's in the Veneto, we will touch of a few of the key area.
❖ Major regions / areas of for discussion will include the following.
  - ➤ Soave
    - Garganega is the key grape in this area and is the backbone for most of the Soave along with Trebbiano. Chardonnay will also make its way into the blend. The better quality wines will have less Trebbiano. Having said that, there is a lot of just so so wines and Soave has received its fair share on remarks.
  - ➤ Valpolicella (meaning "valley of many cellars"
    - As described in Tuscany, there is the original and the expanded area, producing the "Classico zone" of Valpolicella. There are a few key and unique styles of wine making taking place here with the use of the Corvina grape and to a slightly lesser degree Molinara and Rondinella. The wine styles for the discussion are:
      - Amarone:
        - ◆ Is one of the unique processes developed from the Roman times almost in the same fashion and response to the use of Port or Sherry. In all cases, a means producing a wine with longevity to meet long distance time and travel. The process is to harvest the grapes prior to the standard time frame in the vineyard and place the harvest on straw mats to ripen and dry in the sun. This dehydration process creates an interest character and flavor for the wine. The dehydration alters the water to sugar ratio producing a sweeter available <u>must</u> and the sun baking gives the end wine a raisin like nose and palate. The result is a higher alcoholic wine with a sweet like wine but not sweet. The wine takes on a coffee, tar, spice, cherry quality about it.
      - Recioto:
        - ◆ Recioto comes about in the same manner as Amarone, same grapes and harvesting process and use of straw mates to dry (the drying time is usually a bit longer) but the deviation is to arrest the fermentation before exhausting the

residing sugar. The outcome in a very sweet wine with the same characteristic of the Amarone version. Often students confess reminiscence of cough syrup.

➢ Bordolono
  ▪ Along Lake Garda Bordolino produces dry and light reds from primarily made from the Corvina, Rondinello and Molinara grapes.

❖ **Leading Wines**
  ➢ **Amarone and Recioto**
  ➢ **Prosecco:**
    ▪ This is the sparkling wine that is unique to this region versus the Spumante or Frizzante that is produce throughout Italy. This is often confusing but this is a region as well as the varietal and unique to the Veneto zone. The process of Prosecco is produce by what is called the Charmat method (cuvee close).
  ➢ **Soave** (made with Garganega and Trebbiano)
  ➢ **Valpolicella**
    ▪ A style for Recioto(sweet) and Amarone (Dry)
      • Grapes:
        ◆ Corvina
        ◆ Rondinella
        ◆ Molinara

❖ **Grapes for this region:**
  ➢ <u>Whites</u>
    ▪ Chardonnay
    ▪ Garganega
    ▪ Pinot Bianco
    ▪ Pinot Grigio
    ▪ Prosecco (sparkling wines)
    ▪ Tocai Friulano
    ▪ Trebbiano (Soave)
    ▪ Vespaiola (the name comes from the warps that feast on it at harvest time).
  ➢ <u>Reds</u>
    ▪ Cabernet Sauvignon
    ▪ Corvina
    ▪ Merlot
    ▪ Molinara
    ▪ Negrara
    ▪ Rondinella

GRAPES: OF NORTH-WESTERN ITALY

RED	WHITE
NEBBIOLO	CORTESE
BARBERA	ARNEIS
DOLCETTO	MOSCATO
BRACHETTO	ALBANA
LAMBRUSCA	CHARDONNAY
PINOT NOIR	

ITALY: KEY APPELLATIONS DISCUSSED IN REGION:

NORTH-WESTERN
*Piedmont
   *Barolo
   *Barberesco
   *Barbera d'Alba
   *Ghemme
   *Gattinara
   *Dolcetto
   *Brachetto d'Acqui
   *Asti
   *Cortese di Gavi
   *Moscatto d'Asti

SOIL: Volcanic; Limestone; Gravelly Clay.

CLIMATE: Mostly Mediterranean

QUALITY CONTROLS AND LAWS:
- Vino da Tavola (VdT)
- Indicazione Geografica Tipica (IGT)
- Donominazione di Origine Controllata (DOC)
- Donominazione di Origine
- Controllata Garantita(DOCG)

The Donominazione di Origine Controllata Laws provide four different levels for NORTH-WESTERN

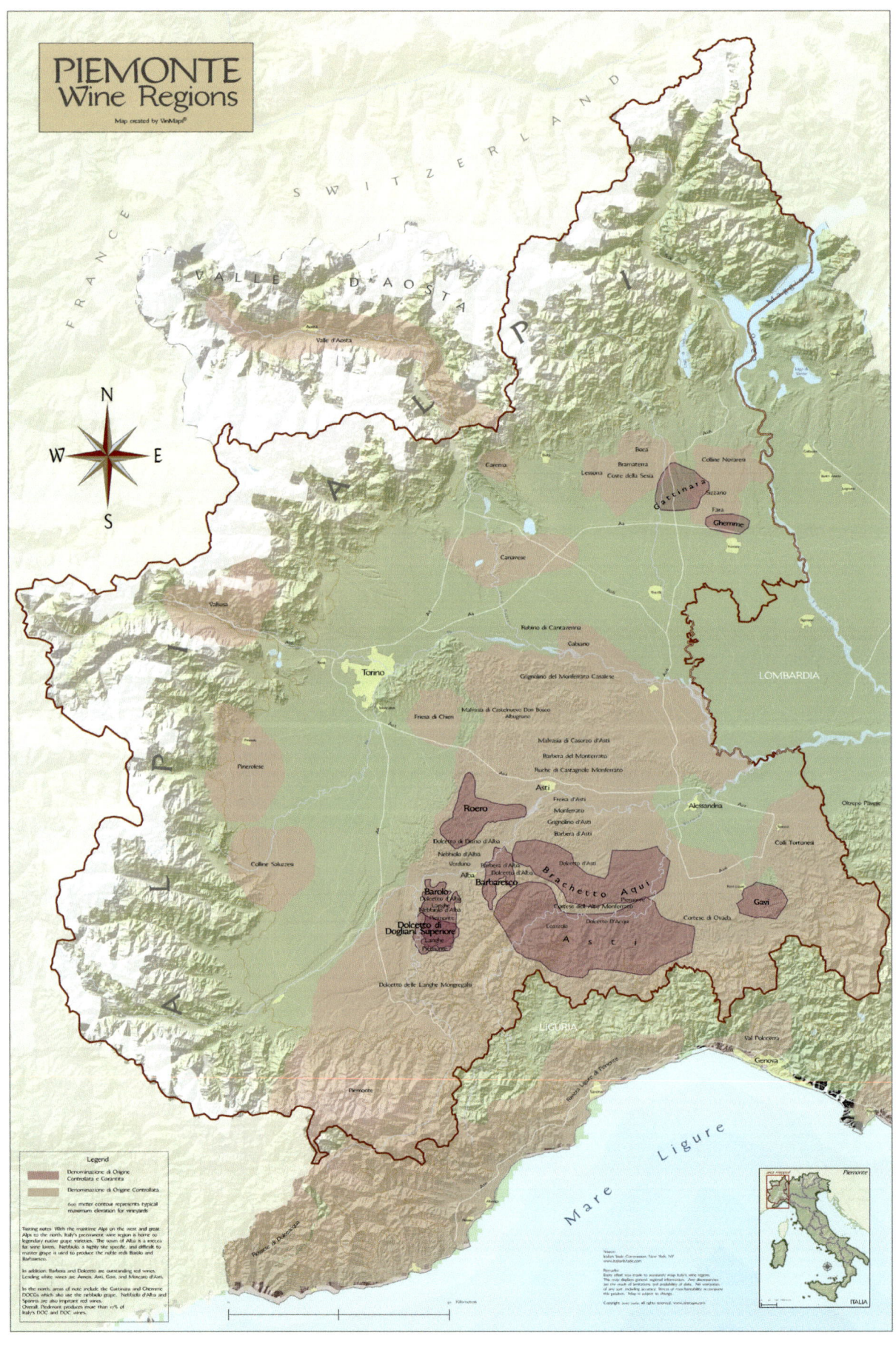

North- West Italy

- ❖ Piemonte
  - ▪ Piedmont (means => foot of the mountains)
  - ▪ Spanna … another name for Nebbiolo in non DOC areas
  - ▪ Nebbiolo=> meaning Fog
  - ▪ Piedmont and Burgundy share the philosophic belief that great wine is the progeny of a single, perfectly adapted grape variety (Nebbiolo in Piedmont; Pinot Noir in Burgundy)
  - ▪ This large region in north-west Italy is, as its name suggests, surrounded by mountains. It is the most important Italian region for the tradition of quality wines.

- ➢ Barolo
  - ▪ *Barolo (red) Langhe Hills
    - • This renowned red wine, named for a village south-west of Alba, comes from the Nebbiolo grape grown in 2900 acres of vineyards in the steep Langhe hills, Barolo's status as "king of wines and wine of kings" for a time proved to be more of a burden than a benefit among Italians who considered its austere power too much for modern palates. Barolo's are said to still be in its infancy state after a decade of aging. These wines are big and long lived.
- ➢ Barbaresco
  - ▪ *Barbaresco (red)
    - • This prestigious red wine, grown near Alba in the Langhe hills south-east of Turin, is often linked with its neighbor Barolo as the noblest example of the Nebbiolo grape. Barbaresco tends to be a shade softer and less powerful. So if Barolo is the King, then Barbaresco takes on the Queen status. The wine usually takes less time to mature only one year of wood aging is required as opposed to Barolo's 2years and is often considered the most approachable of the two, as exemplified by the international style of Gaja. The zone covers about 1100 acres of vineyards in the communes of Barbaresco. Gaja makes very long- lived wines (20 years or more), but all good examples will last at least a decade.
- ➢ Gattinara
  - ▪ Gattinara can be a hit or miss and is capable of great and not so great wines. Situated in northern Piedmont and elevated to DOCG in the past few years. The use of the Nebbiolo grapes in Gattinara produces softer and lighter wines than Barolo or Barbaresco but still produce delicious, black plums, tar and roses flavor.
- ➢ Ghemme
  - ▪ *Ghemme nebbiolo (can seem to be a mini Barolo)
  - ▪ A red, Nebbiolo- based wine produced on the opposite bank of the Sésia River to Gattinara. Ghemme can often surpass its better known neighbor in style and certainly has its moments. Wines can age similarly to Gattinara, generally up to 10 years.
- ➢ Carema
  - ▪ *Carema (from the Nebbiolo and more north in Piedmont)

- Tiny quantities of wine trickle from the Nebbiolo vines grown on the steep, rocky slopes of this small zone in the northern Piedmont. Lighter than many other Nebbiolos, these wines can have great elegance and perfume. Production is confined to two good producers, the cantina sociale, and Luigi Ferrando. Cantina Sociale (so-charle) Italian for co-op, accounting for about 60% of Italian wine production.

➢ Asti
  - *Asti (sparkling and sweet)
    • Asti Spumante, the world's best selling sweet sparkling wine is made in the province of Asti south-east of Turin, and was for a long associated with a light and cheap style of wine, and have struggled to escape that association even after being promoted to a DOCG status and recognizing quality. Under the new appellation which includes superior Moscato d'Asti, the wine may be simply called, Asti without the spumante to avoid confusion with other sparklers.

➢ Gavi
  - *Gavi (Cortese) (white)
    • An expensive and still overrated white made from the cortese grape. This wine can age 5 years or more. Steely, Lemon characteristic made in the southern eastern part of Piedmont.. Can be labeled as simply Cortese del Piemonte.

➢ Brachetto d' Acqui / Acqui
  - The region falls under the hills of Monferrato just southeast of Asti. The key town is Acqui.
    • Grape: Brachetto

➢ Barbera (DOC)
  - Barbera d'Alba (red) (Barbera grape)
    • Some of the most outstanding Barbera comes from this appellation. Many producers of Barolo and Barbaresco have in addition to prized Nebbiolo, have portioned a part of their vineyards with Barbera. Much of this variety is relegated to the lowest or more easterly slopes. Having said that it can perform at least as well as Nebbiolo over a wide area that includes Barolo, Barbaresco and Roero hills

➢ Dolcetto (DOC)
  - Dolcetto d'Alba (red) (dolcetto; meaning little sweet one)
    • This is the most important zone in north-west Italy for Dolcetto, which .includes the hills of Barolo and Barbaresco. The soil is calcareous and the climate conditions are conducive for this early ripening variety. Low acid, tannin and lighter body.
    • Dolcetto wines are produced under seven different DOC classifications. This is not uncommon with other regions as well.

GRAPES: OF CENTRAL ITALY

RED	WHITE
SANGIOVESE	VERNACCIA
CANAIOLO	VERMENTINO
CABERNET SAUVIGNON	MALVASIA
MERLOT	TREBBIANO

ITALY: KEY APPELLATIONS DISCUSSED IN REGION:

CENTRAL ITALY
*Tuscany
- Brunello di Montalcino
- Carmignano
- Chianti
- Chianti Classico
- Vernaccia di San Gimignano
- Vino Nobile de Montepulciano

SOIL: Limestone; Gravelly Clay.

CLIMATE: Moderate Maritime

QUALITY CONTROLS AND LAWS:
- Vino da Tavola (VdT)
- Indicazione Geografica Tipica (IGT)
- Donominazione di Origine Controllata (DOC)
- Donominazione di Origine Controllata Garantita(DOCG)

The Donominazione di Origine Controllata Laws provide four different levels for
CENTRAL ITALY

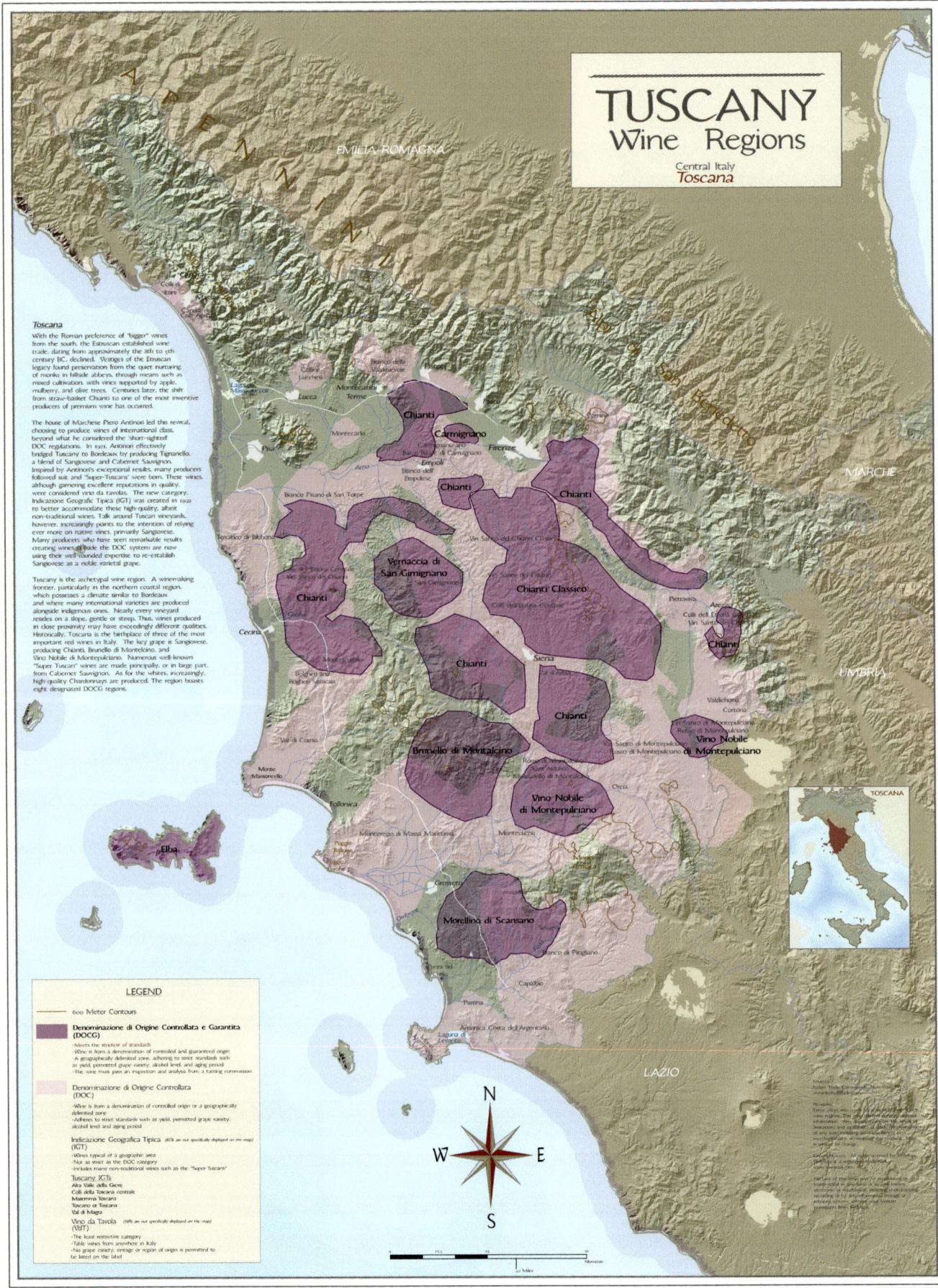

TUSCANY
Wine Regions
Central Italy
Toscana

Toscana

With the Roman preference of "bigger" wines from the south, the Etruscan established wine trade, dating from approximately the 8th to 9th century BC, declined. Vestiges of the Etruscan legacy found preservation from the quiet nurturing of monks in hillside abbeys, through means such as mixed cultivation, with vines supported by apple, mulberry, and olive trees. Centuries later, the shift from straw-basket Chianti to one of the most inventive producers of premium wine has occurred.

The house of Marchese Piero Antinori led this revival, choosing to produce wines of international class, beyond what he considered the "short-sighted" DOC regulations. In 1971, Antinori effectively bridged Tuscany to Bordeaux by producing Tignanello, a blend of Sangiovese and Cabernet Sauvignon. Inspired by Antinori's exceptional results, many producers followed suit and "Super-Tuscans" were born. These wines, although garnering excellent reputations in quality, were considered vino da tavola. The new category, Indicazione Geografica Tipica (IGT) was created in 1992 to better accommodate these high-quality, albeit non-traditional wines. Talk around Tuscan vineyards, however, increasingly points to the intention of relying ever more on native vines, primarily Sangiovese. Many producers who have seen remarkable results creating wines outside the DOC system are now using their well-rounded expertise to re-establish Sangiovese as a noble varietal grape.

Tuscany is the archetypal wine region. A winemaking frontier, particularly in the northern coastal region, which possesses a climate similar to Bordeaux and where many international varieties are produced alongside indigenous ones. Nearly every vineyard resides on a slope, gentle or steep. Thus, wines produced in close proximity may have exceedingly different qualities. Historically, Toscana is the birthplace of three of the most important red wines in Italy. The key grape is Sangiovese, producing Chianti, Brunello di Montalcino, and Vino Nobile di Montepulciano. Numerous well-known "Super Tuscan" wines are made principally, or in large part, from Cabernet Sauvignon. As for the whites, increasingly, high-quality Chardonnays are produced. The region boasts eight designated DOCG regions.

LEGEND

— 600 Meter Contours

Denominazione di Origine Controllata e Garantita (DOCG)
- Meets the strictest of standards
- Wine is from a denomination of controlled and guaranteed origin
- A geographically delimited zone, adhering to strict standards such as yield, permitted grape variety, alcohol level, and aging period
- The wine must pass an inspection and analysis from a tasting commission

Denominazione di Origine Controllata (DOC)
- Wine is from a denomination of controlled origin or a geographically delimited zone
- Adheres to strict standards such as yield, permitted grape variety, alcohol level and aging period

Indicazione Geografica Tipica (80% are not specifically displayed on the map) **(IGT)**
- Wines typical of a geographic area
- Not as strict as the DOC category
- Includes many non-traditional wines such as the "Super Tuscans"

Tuscany IGTs
Alta Valle della Greve
Colli della Toscana centrale
Maremma Toscana
Toscano or Toscana
Val di Magra

Vino da Tavola (80% are not specifically displayed on the map) **(VdT)**
- The least restrictive category
- Table wines from anywhere in Italy
- No grape variety, vintage or region of origin is permitted to be listed on the label

Central Italy

- ❖ **Tuscany / Toscana**

- ➢ DOCG:
- ➢ When you think Tuscany you think Chianti and indeed this is one of the best and well known wines of Italy and the world. There are actually three of the best and most known wines in this region
  - ▪ Chianti / Chianti Classico
  - ▪ Brunello di Montalcino
  - ▪ Vino Nobile di Montepulciano
- ➢ Having listed the three, it is difficult not to mention the bis Super-Tuscans that are derived from Bordeaux varietals.
- ➢ **Brunello di Montalcino**
  - ▪ Famous Tuscan zone south of Siena, traditionally noted for high wine prices and dark, impenetrable flavors from the Sangiovese (aka Brunello) grape.
    - • Grape: Sangiovese

- ➢ **Carmignano**
  - ▪ Red wine from the Montalbano hills west of Florence renowned since the 16th century and revived in the 1960's Ugo Contini Bonacossi of Capezzana. Arguing that Cabernet had been planted in Carmignano in the 18th century, he brought back cuttings from Lafite in Bordeaux for his own vineyards. The blend (85% Sangiovese / 15% Cabernet) is one of the Tuscany's more refined wines and can be very long live.
    - • Grapes:
      - ◆ Red: Sangiovese, Canaiolo Nero, Cabernet Franc

- ➢ **Chianti**
- ➢ Their is Chianti and Chianti Classico: The original area of Chianti produced Sangiovese since the middle ages and it was not until much later that politics and profit came into play with the proposal to expand the Chianti region. Those existing within the region were against the idea and those outside were in favor, the sort of it, government legislation won out. Those that were apart of the original, rename Chianti to Chianti Classico reflecting the original Chianti for those that truly want to differentiate the two. In terms of talking "Terrior" here is a clear example of Terrior recognized for Sangiovese and expanding this region of unlike soil composition take preference of unique and original soil boundaries.
  - ▪ Chianti is the most famous of all Italian wines, but there are many Chianti styles, depending on which grapes are used, where they are grown, and by which producer.
    - • Grapes:
      - ◆ Red: Sangiovese, Cabernet Sauvignon, Merlot
      - ◆ White: Trebbiano, Vermentino

➢ **Chianti Classico**
  ▪ The modern Chianti Classico zone is based on the historic Chianti boundaries though, regrettably, it now includes a large tract of unsuitable heavy clay soils in the north and north-west. However many of the best
  ▪ Tuscany are to be found here. From the 1995 vintage, Classico can be 100% Sangiovese and the riserva needs to be aged for only 2 years, instead of 3.
    • Grapes:
      ◆ Red: Sangiovese, Cabernet Sauvignon, Merlot
      ◆ White: Trebbiano, Vermentino

➢ **Vernaccia di San Gimignano**
  ▪ The dry white wine made from the Vernaccia grape grown in the hills around the beautiful Tuscan town of San Gimignano gained fame as Italy's first DOC in 1966. This fame was perhaps justified then when every other Tuscan white wine was made with Trebbiano.

➢ **Vino Nobile di Montepulciano**
  ▪ The noble wine from the hills around the town of Montepulciano is made from the Sangiovese grape, known locally as the Prugnolo, with the help of a little Canaiolo and Mammolo. At its best, it combines the power and structure of Brunello di Montalcino with the finesse and complexity found in the best Chianti Classico.
    • Grapes:
      ◆ Red: Sangiovese (Prugnolo), Canaiolo,

➢ **Super-Tuscans wine**
  ▪ A good time to talk about some of the bigger and hardier wines of Central Italy. To answer the called of competing with the North – West (Barolos and Barbarescos) the Super- Tuscan came into play. This is the blending of Sangiovese varietal with one of the Bordeaux varietals such as Cabernet Sauvignon. The Cab would add the needed backbone to the otherwise lighter and softer Chianti. Within the Laws, the use of Bordeaux or non Italian varietals could not hold a greater title than IGT. So the first non Italian varietal Super-Tuscan was born called Sassicaia. A blend of Cabernet Sauvignon and Cabernet Franc, Later Ornellaia came into play with a blend of Cabernet Sauvignon, Merlot and some Cabernet Franc.
  ▪ The Super-Tuscans are given fantasy names such as; Sassicaia, Ornellaia, Tignanello, etc. All can vary with the use of Bordeaux varietals and or not including Sangiovese. It wasn't until much later and from great effort that a DOC status was achieved for this wine to a particular location.

GRAPES: OF SOUTHERN ITALY

RED	WHITE
AGLIANICO	GRECO
NEGROAMARO	VERDELLO
CANNONAU	VERMENTINO

ITALY: KEY APPELLATIONS DISCUSSED IN REGION:

SOUTHERN ITALY

Puglia (Apulia)
  Salice Salentino
Campania
  Taurasi
Basilicata
  Aglianico de Vulture
Sicily
  Marsala
Sardinia
  Vermention di Galluria

SOIL: Volcanic; Limestone; Gravelly Clay.

CLIMATE: Continental Mostly

QUALITY CONTROLS AND LAWS:
- Vino da Tavola (VdT)
- Indicazione Geografica Tipica (IGT)
- Donominazione di Origine Controllata (DOC)
- Donominazione di Origine
- Controllata Garantita(DOCG)

The Donominazione di Origine Controllata Laws provide four different levels for Southern Italy

Southern Italy

- ➤ Southern Italy and Sicily
- ➤ **Campania:** The key area here is Taurasi (DOCG) and the Mastroberardino winery (use of Aglianico). The region of Maples and Vesuvius and been known for its desert wines, and there is "Monrevetrano" which is a blend of Cabernet Sauvignon, Merlot and Aglianico.
  - ▪ Grapes:
    - • Red: Cabernet Sauvignon, Merlot and Aglianico.
    - • White: Greco

- ➤ **Puglia:** There are no DOCG's in Pulgia. This is the heel of the southern region, which forms the heel of the Italian boot, offering a large array of blending wines.
  - ▪ **Grapes:**
    - • Red: Negroamaro, Malvasia Nera and Primitivo
    - • White: Chardonnay, Malvasia Blanca and Verdeca

- ➤ **Basilicata:** This southern Italian region, producing huge reds. The popular grape here again is Aglianico that is grown on the steep slopes of Mt Vulture an extinct Volcano. In addition to the Aglianico, sparkling Moscato is produce here as well.
  - ▪ Grape:
    - • Red: Aglianico
    - • White: Malvasia, Muscato

- ➤ **Calabria:** The toe of Italy is one of its poorest regions. In the past Cirò DOC was the wine offered to champions in the ancient Olympics and gave it some status. Much Ciro is made from the Gaglioppo grape.
  - ▪ Grape:
    - • Red: Gaglioppo, Magliocco
    - • White: Greco, Montonico

- ➤ **Sicilia: Sicily:** It is very hot on the island, and the traditional wines are the high in alcohol. The fortified wine (Marsala) derived from the Arab phase marsah-el-Allah or "port of God". The wines are categorized according to three variables: their color, their age, and their sweetness level.
  - ▪ **Grapes:**
    - • Red: Nero D' Avola
    - • White: Catarratto, Grillo (base for Marsala)

- ➤ **Marsala**
  - ▪ Fine: age 1 year and not necessarily in wood, used for cooking
  - ▪ Superiore: aged min of 2 years; 4 years for riserva in large oak or chestnut casks

- Vergine or Soleras: most complex and longest aged of the three, requiring a Minimun of 5 years in wood and riserva minimum of 10 years.
- Fine & Superiore : can be made
  - Secco (dry)
  - Semisecco (off dry)
  - Dolce (sweet)

- **Sardegna (Sardinia**) : This is a hilly Mediterranean island with grapes of Spanish origin as well as native.
  - Grapes:
    - White Vermentino and Torbato
      - Malvasia of Greek origin
      - Vernaccia of Native origin
    - Red: Connonau and Carignano

SPAIN: KEY APPELLATIONS DISCUSSED IN REGION:

North – Western
- Galicia
- Rias Baixas
- Ribeiro

The North Central
- Navarra
- Castilla y Leon
- Ribero del Duero
- Rueda

Rioja

North – Eastern
- Cataluna
  - Penedes
  - Priorato

The Sothern Region
- Andalucia
  - Jerez

GRAPES OF SPAIN: WILL BE COVERED IN EACH REGION

QUALITY CONTROLS AND LAWS:
- Vino De Mesa (VdM)
- Vino De La Tierra (VdT)
- Donominación de Origen (DO)
- Donominación de Origen Calificada (DOC)

The Donominación de Origen Laws provide four different levels levels SPAIN

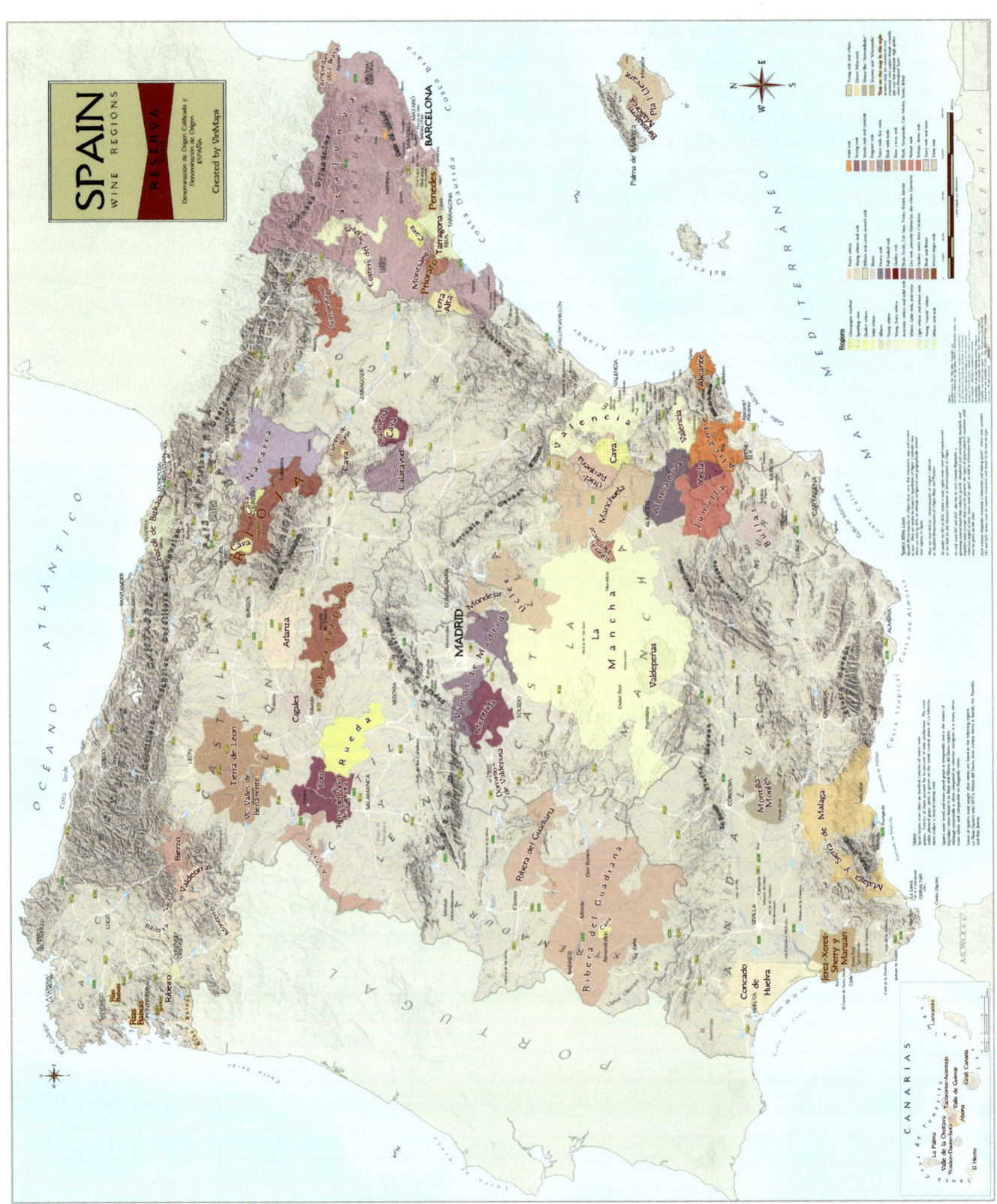

Spain

- ➤ **Spain's Wine Laws**
  - The Spanish Denominacion de Origen (DO) laws, first enacted in 1932 and revised in 1970, are similar to France's Appellation d'Origine Controlee laws, which define and protect wines from specific geographic areas. There are 60 DO's now officially recognized and geographically defined, in Spain. In addition, Rioja was the Only Denominacion de Origen Calificado (DOC) 1991, or Qualified Denomination of Origen. Since then, Priorato has gained the same status as of July 2009
    - *These are set forth by the National Institute of Denominations of Origen.
  - Consejo Regulador
  - Vino da Mesa (VdT)
  - Vino de la Tierra (VdlT)
  - Donominazione di Origine
  - Donominazione di Origine Calificada (DOC)

GRAPES: NORTH-WESTERN OF SPAIN:

RED	WHITE
CAIŃO TINTO	ALBARIŃO
MENCIA	TREIXADURA
	TORRONTÉS

SPAIN: KEY APPELLATIONS DISCUSSED IN REGION:

North – Western
- Galicia
  - Rias Baixas
  - Ribeiro

SOIL: Mostly Alluvial, Granite

Climate: Damp Mediterranean

QUALITY CONTROLS AND LAWS:
- Vino da Mesa (VdT)
- Vino Comarcal (VC)
- Vino de la Tierra (VdlT)
- Donominazione di Origine

The Donominación de Origen Laws provide different levels North-Western SPAIN

North-Western Spain

❖ **Galicia:** This is a rather damp climate and by nature one of the greenest and coolest areas of Spain. The grape here is Albariño which is the same grape known as Alvarinho of vinho verde in northern Portugal. The key areas to remember here are, Rias Baixas and Ribeiro, which are sub-regions of the Galicia area. The wines are reminiscent of white peach and green apple with often a bit of CO_2 that gives it liveliness with the local seafood.

➢ **Ribeiro:**
- This is an area that has utilized the Palomino grape for quite sometime. Although the key grape for Sherry in the southern region, it is used for still wines in Ribeiro. Eventually the Palomino was replaced with a grape varietal called Treixadura and the other Torrontés (also found in the northern part of Argentina). The grapes here make fairly light styles wines utilizing the new cold fermentation techniques that are now available.
  - o Grapes: Treixadure, Torrontes, and some Palomino

➢ Rías Baixas
- Also produce much of the white wine for this Northern region. Rías Baixas relies heavily on the Albarino for its production. These wines are 100% albarino if labeled on the bottle. If the region appears (Rías Baixas) then at least 70% Albariño must be present in the blend.
  - • Grapes: Albariño

GRAPES OF SPAIN:

RED	WHITE
TEMPRANILLO	VERDEJO
GARNACHA	SAUVIGNON BLANC
CABERNET SAUVIGNON	GARNACHA BLANC
GRACIANO	VIURA
MAZEULO	MALVASIA

SPAIN: KEY APPELLATIONS DISCUSSED IN REGION:

The North Central
   Navarra
Castilla y Leon
   Ribero del Duero
   Rueda
Rioja

SOIL: Calcareous Clay, Alluvial

CLIMATE: Continental

QUALITY CONTROLS AND LAWS:

- Vino da Mesa (VdT)
- Vino de la Tierra (VdlT)
- Donominazione di Origine
- Donominazione di Origine Calificada (DOC)

The Donominazione di Origine Controllata Laws provide four different levels NORTH - CENTRAL SPAIN

- ❖ **NORTHERN-CENTRAL SPAIN**
  - ➢ **Navarra:**
    - ▪ Navarra is a single province from the foothills of Pyrenees to Rioja. Actually small portion of Navarra included in a part of Rioja. As with most of Spain the climate is dry, arid and far enough inland to be continental.
      - • 90% of all wine comes from co-operatives
      - • Grape:
        - ◆ Red: Garnacha, Merlot, Cabernet Sauvignon
        - ◆ White: Viura, Chardonnay
  - ➢ **Castilla León:**
    - ▪ The language is Castillian. This is a very large area covering most of the North Central part of Spain. Much credit is due to Vega Sicilia which was established in the 1900's.
    - ▪ Grapes:
      - • Red: Tinto del Pais, Garnacha Tinta, Merlot, Cabernet Sauvignon
      - • White: Verdejo and Sauvignon Blanc
    - ▪ There are five DO's in this region but the two at this point to focus on are:
  - ➢ **Ribera del Duero**
    - ▪ About 80 miles north of Madrid. Nearly exclusively RED wine region. About 100 estates in Ribera del Duero. Tinto Fino, aka Tinto del Pais, aka Tempranillo. Tempranillo take its name from Temprano: meaning (early) and indeed the grape is early ripening in the season. Ribera del Duero is named after the river Duero that crosses the central part of Spain to Portugal. Ribera is about ¼ the size of the vineyards in Rioja. Long time aging as is Rioja.
    - ▪ Grapes: Tempranillo, Cabernet Sauvignon, Garnacha
    - ▪ **Ribera Del Duero:** now rivals the renowned Rioja. Ribera Del Duero received DO status in 1982 and is now on the cusp of a DOC status. The key grape here is Tempranillo better known locally as Tinto Roriz. This is a good time to note that the famous Tempranillo varietal will have at least a dozen AKA's throughout Spain, including Portugal.
    - ▪ Make note: a major Player on the western edge of this region is the famous wine producer Vega Sicilia, making wine for over a 100 years. The Bodega that sparked a Revolution.
  - ➢ **Rueda:**
    - ▪ Rueda is the most southerly DO, moving south from the Duero River is the other key region to know well at this point. Rueda received its status in 1980. The key grape here is Verdejo, clean crisp high acid and citrusy wine. Rueda is major for white wines and we should cover some of the key issues and regulations with this. There are five types of white wine produced.
      - • **Rueda** wines must have a minimum of 50% Verdejo.
      - • **Rueda Verdejo** must contain a minimum of 85% verdejo.
      - • **Rueda Sauvignon Blanc** must be that varietal completely.
      - • **Rueda Espumoso** is a sparkling wine and must have 50% Verdejo
      - • **Rueda Dorado** must like sherry must be aged for a min of 3 years with a alcohol strength of at least 15%.

- Grapes:
  - Red: Tempranillo, Cabernet Sauvignon, Merlot, Garnacha
  - White: Viura, Verdejo, Sauvignon Blanc
- Make note a major player in this region is the renown Marqués de Riscal.

❖ **Rioja** (Spain's preeminent wine region)
  - Rioja is North Center of Spain. In general, Riojo's red wines are aged longer before release than any other wines in the world
  - Often thought of as Spain's Bordeaux, many of the wines have a delicacy more reminiscent of Burgundy.
  - In 1780 a Riojo wine-maker named Manuel Quintano adoted this oak barrel aging method, that well be discussed shortly
    - *In 1901 Phylloxera crept in and destroyed 70% of the vineyards.
  - There are three sub-region of Rioja that should be noted and committed to memory.
    - Rioja Alta
    - Rioja Alavesa
    - Rioja Baja
    - Grapes:
      - Red: Garnacha, Graciano, Mazuelo (carignan), Tempranillo
      - White: Garnacha Blanca, Malvasia, Viura

- Interesting Note: The Original wine cooler…. Spanish punch of wine and citrus juice. Called Sant'gria (Santiago and Sangria). This was shown in New York trade show and eventually purchased by Pepsi – Cola. Renamed Yago Sant'gria. Pepsi ultimately bought the entire Rioja Santiago Bodega.

Styles of the Riojo related to **Oak Aging**

➤ **Joven → Crianza → Reserva → Gran Reserva**

➤ **Classified according to the quality and aging**:
➤ **Joven:** no oak aging or very little (that is would not qualify as a Crianza) with this particular style. Joven: meaning (child, child-like, basically young wine) are wines that are released to be drunk young.
➤ **Crianza:** the youngest; in Spanish the word refers to something that is raised of nursed. Other might also be called **(vinos joven or sin crianza).**
  - *reds:** must be aged for at least 2 years, one of which must be in oak barrels.
  - *whites:** must be aged for 6 months in oak barrels
➤ **Reserva:** made from superior grapes from prime sites, reserves are more that just simple fruity wines.
  - *reds:** must be aged for at least 3 years, one of which must be in oak barrels.
  - *whites:** must be aged for 1 year, 6 months of which must be in oak barrels

➢ **Gran Reservas:** made only in exceptional years, come from the very best vineyards of all and are extremely rare. In most years, Gran Reservas represent just 1 to 10 % of the wines produced.

- ▪ **Reds:** must be aged for at least 5 years, two of which must be in oak barrels and the remaining 3 years of which must be in bottles. Recent changes now permit 4 ½ years.
- ▪ **Whites:** must be aged for 4 years, six months of which must be in oak barrels.

➢ Riojo bottles are sometimes wrapped in protective lattice of thin wire called (net) or malla (mesh). This practice dates from the 19th century prior to Consejo Regulador; when bodegas sought to prevent … misdoings, as in theft of a well aged 5 years old wine and replaced with a lesser.

GRAPES OF SPAIN:

RED	WHITE
GARNACHA	PARELLADA
CARIŃENA	MACABEO
	XAREL-LO
	VIURA
	CHARDONNAY

SPAIN: KEY APPELLATIONS DISCUSSED IN REGION:

North – Eastern
- Cataluna
  - Penedes
  - Priorato

SOIL: Limestone, Chalk

CLIMATE: MEDITERRANEAN

QUALITY CONTROLS AND LAWS:
- Vino da Mesa (VdT)
- Vino de la Tierra (VdlT)
- Donominazione di Origine
- Donominazione di Origine Calificada (DOC)

The Donominazione di Origine Controllata Laws provide four different levels NORTH - EASTERN SPAIN

North — Eastern Spain

- This is Cava (sparkling wine) country. The sparkling wines are made in the same method or tradition (Méthode Champenoise) as in Champagne France. As with Spain and other countries most mimic the name of Champagne and wanted to convey the same style, process and quality of Champagne. Spain as with the other countries, acquiesced to another name for the bubbly.
- **Cataluña / Catalunya; Penedes; and Priorat:**
  - Are the key areas in the North-Eastern part of Spain
- **Cataluña / Catalunya** is the all encompassing region and DO and still remains the heart of Cava.
  - **Key Grapes to remember for Cava are:**
    - Parellada
    - Macabeo
    - Xarel-lo
- **Penedes**
  - Just south-west of Barcelona and under the influence of the Mediterranean Coast is Penedes. The vineyards supply most of the grapes for Cava production. In addition to the more well know cava varietals other varietals are:
    - Grapes:
      - Red: Garnacha, Monanstrell, Pinot Noir, Cariñena
      - White: Gewurztraminer, Chardonnay, Riesling
- **Priorat or (Priorato) DOC**
  - This is the very new DOC of Spain, just recently approved as of June 2009. Priorat now joins Rioja as a DOC's. Priorat has gained a great deal of attention and now boost some of the greatest wines on unique soil known as llicorella (layers of red slate and mica)
  - Grapes:
    - Red: Garnacha, Cariñena (also known elsewhere in Spain as Mazuelo), Cabernet Sauvignon, Syrah and Pinot Noir.

  - The use of long aging in Oak barrels and often the use of the Solera system.

GRAPES OF SPAIN:
RED   WHITE
PALOMINO
PEDRO XIMÉNEZ   MOSCATEL

SPAIN: KEY APPELLATIONS
DISCUSSED IN REGION:

The Sothern Region
- Andalucia
  - Jerez

SOIL: Porous chalky soils

CLIMATE: Most Continental

QUALITY CONTROLS AND LAWS:
- Vino da Mesa (VdT)
- Vino de la Tierra (VdlT)
- Donominazione di Origine

The Laws provide three different levels southern
SPAIN

Southern Spain

❖ **Jerez**

➢ Sherry is the England term
➢ Xérès is the French term
➢ **Sherry** is the an abused named adopted by bulk winemakers in various parts of the world to describe cheap, inferior wines, although within European union, its usage is limited to Spanish Sherry as of the 1st of 1996. Actual (real) Sherry comes from the triangle of Vineyard land between Andalusian of inland Jerez, and Sanlúcar de Barrameda and Puerto de Santa Maria by the sea.

  ▪ Natural yeast called "Flor" builds up on the sherry and must be aged minimum of 3 years old. But fine Sherries age in barrels for much longer.
  ▪ Most Sherries are blended through a Solera system.
  ▪ Sherry unlike Port is fermented completely dry and if fortified, the Brandy is added after fermentation is completed. If any additional sweetness is desired, a unfermented sweet grape juice is also added after fermentation is completely. The sweet unfermented grape juice is made from the Pedro Ximénez grape or Moscatel.
  ▪ Soil: The soil is to be noted here due to the uniqueness of it. There are three types
    • Albariza: is the finest of all, taking on the appearance of snow (60%- 80% chalk). This is the most important and what most vineyard are made of.
    • Barro: is brown / reddish in appearance cause by the presence of Iron, a small amount is chalk.
    • Arena: is the other type, consisting of a sandy, yellowish / reddish aspect, again due to iron.
  ▪ Styles:
    • **Fino:** youngest…flor protects from air.
    • **Manzanillas**: a Fino style that has aged longer in cooler area of Sanlúcar de Barrameda where the flor grows thickest.
    • **Amontillados:** are Fino Sherries that continued their ages after the flor has died about 6 to 8 years. And therefore continued their aging in air contact. These should all be bone dry.
    • **Olorosos:** (sweet or dry) is fortified after fermentation to deter the growth of Flor. Olorosos therefore mature in barrels in contact with air. Producing a very dark, rich and intensely nutty flavors.

❖ **Mistela**: unfermented grape juice that is fortified and added to Sherry as a sweetner.

❖ Other styles: Palo Cortado…quite rare in style it falls
❖ between Amontillado and Olorosos… but not Fino or Olorosos.
❖ The Solera system
  ▪ Is a means to making Sherry aged wines. A bodega will have back years of barrels that are then blended forward to the new years. The wine is basically siphoned off the older barrel and blended forward to the next proceeding year it does not have to be consecutive year. The barrels are never completely full and allow space for this type of blending forward. Crianderia is name given for the row of barrels undergoing the solera system, the rows are identified as; first Crianderia, second Crianderia, third Crianderia, etc. The current year is on top. So in summation, the current wine would have the pedigree of multiple prior years. There is no limit as to the number of previous blended years it is usually dependent on the Bodegas available prior years of Sherry.

GRAPES OF PORTUGAL:

RED	WHITE
TOURIGA NATIONALE	ALVARINHO
TINTA RORIZ	MALVASIA (VITAL)
TINTA CÁO	VELDELHO
TINTA BARROCA	

ITALY: KEY
APPELLATIONS
DISCUSSED IN REGION:

PORTUGAL
   Douro
   Bairrada
   Dão
   Vinho Verde
   Ribatejo

SOIL:

CLIMATE: Atlantic Ocean influence; Maritime to Continental for the inland areas.

QUALITY CONTROLS AND LAWS:
- Vino da Mesa (VdT)
- Vinho Regional (VR)
- Indicação de Proveniência Regulamentada (IPR)
- Denominação de Origem Controlada (DOC)
- Garrafeira
- Reserva
- Instituto do Vinho da Madeira (IVM)
- Instituto do Vinho do Porto (IVP)
- Instituto da Vinha e Vinho (IVV)

The Laws and key Terms for levels of PORTUGAL

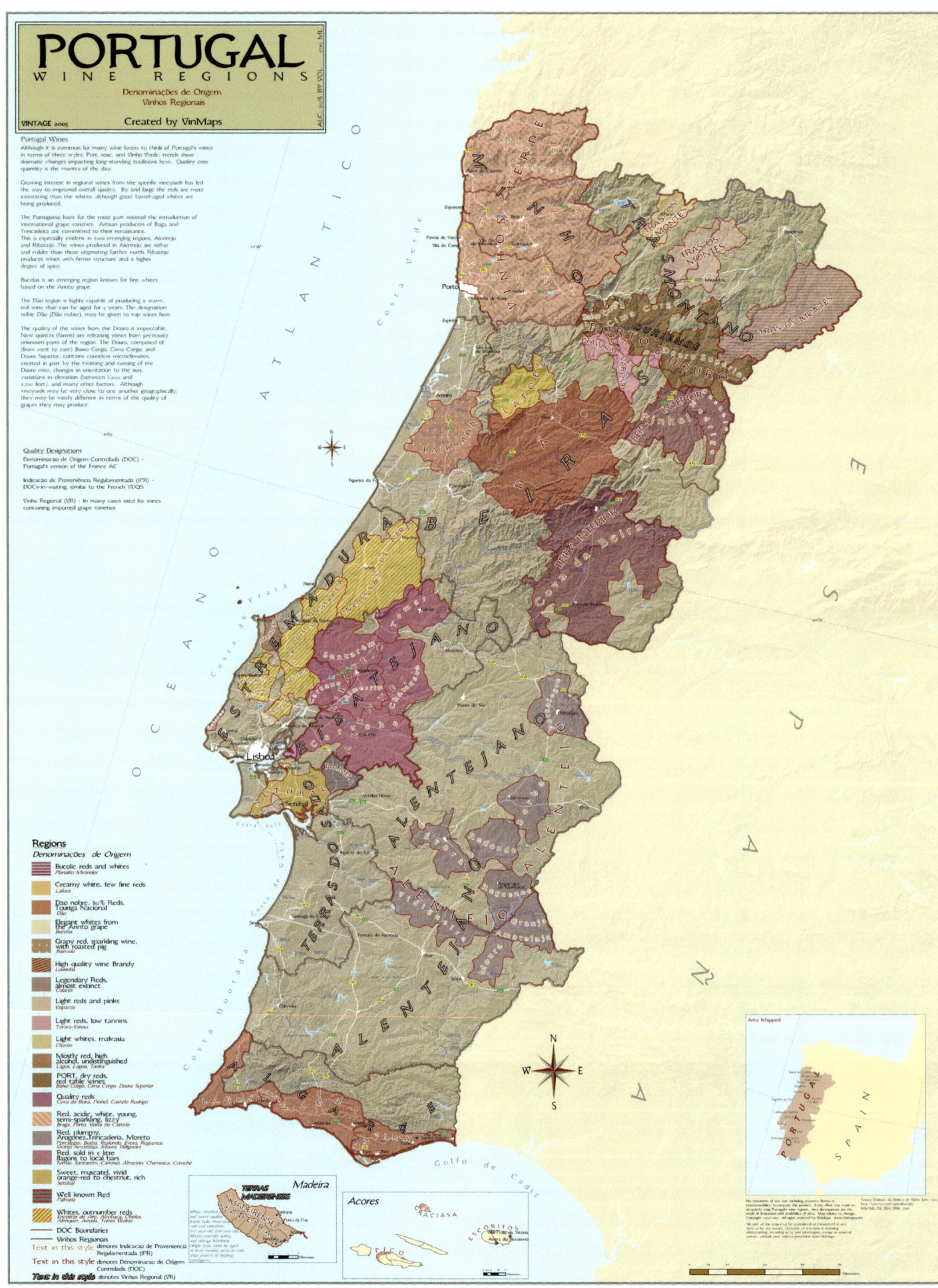

PORTUGAL
W I N E   R E G I O N S
Denominações de Origem
Vinhos Regionais

VINTAGE 2005

Created by VinMaps

Portugal Wines

Although it is common for many wine lovers to think of Portugal's wines in terms of three styles, Port, rose, and Vinho Verde, trends show dramatic changes impacting long-standing traditions here. Quality over quantity is the mantra of the day.

Growing interest in regional wines from site specific vineyards has led the way to improved overall quality. By and large the reds are most interesting than the whites, although good, barrel-aged whites are being produced.

The Portuguese have for the most part resisted the introduction of international grape varieties. Artisan producers of Baga and Trincadeira are committed to their renaissance.
This is especially evident in two emerging regions, Alentejo and Ribatejo. The wines produced in Alentejo are softer and milder than those originating farther north. Ribatejo produces wines with firmer structure and a higher degree of spice.

Bucelas is an emerging region known for fine whites based on the Arinto grape.

The Dão region is highly capable of producing a warm, red wine that can be aged for 5 years. The designation noble Dão (Dão nobre), may be given to top wines here.

The quality of the wines from the Douro is impeccable. New quintas (farms) are releasing wines from previously unknown parts of the region. The Douro, composed of (from west to east) Baixo Corgo, Cima Corgo and Douro Superior, contains countless microclimates, created in part by the twisting and turning of the Douro river. changes in orientation to the sun, variations in elevation (between 1200 and 1700 feet), and many other factors. Although vineyards may be very close to one another geographically, they may be vastly different in terms of the quality of grapes they may produce.

Quality Designations

Denominação de Origem Controlada (DOC) -
Portugal's version of the France AC

Indicação de Proveniência Regulamentada (IPR) -
DOCs-in-waiting, similar to the French VDQS

Vinho Regional (VR) - In many cases used for wines
containing imported grape varieties

Regions
Denominações de Origem

- **Bucolic reds and whites**
  Planalto Mirandês
- **Creamy white, few fine reds**
  Lafões
- **Dão nobre, 80% Reds,**
  Touriga Nacional
  Dão
- **Elegant whites from**
  the Arinto grape
  Bucelas
- **Grapy red, sparkling wine,**
  with roasted pig
  Bairrada
- **High quality wine Brandy**
  Lourinhã
- **Legendary Reds,**
  almost extinct
  Colares
- **Light reds and pinks**
  Valpaços
- **Light reds, low tannins**
  Távora-Varosa
- **Light whites, malvasia**
  Chaves
- **Mostly red, high**
  alcohol, undistinguished
  Lagos, Lagoa, Tavira
- **PORT, dry reds,**
  red table wines
  Baixo Corgo, Cima Corgo, Douro Superior
- **Quality reds**
  Cova da Beira, Pinhel, Castelo Rodrigo
- **Red, acidic, white, young,**
  semi-sparkling, fizzy
  Braga, Porto, Viana do Castelo
- **Red, plummy,**
  Aragonez,Trincaderia, Moreto
  Portalegre, Borba, Redondo, Evora, Reguengos, Granja Amareleja, Moura, Vidigueira
- **Red, sold in 1 litre**
  flagons to local bars
  Tomar, Santarém, Cartaxo, Almeirim, Chamusca, Coruche
- **Sweet, muscatel, vivid**
  orange-red to chestnut, rich
  Setúbal
- **Well known Red**
  Palmela
- **Whites, outnumber reds**
  Encostas de Aire, Alcobaça, Óbidos, Alenquer, Arruda, Torres Vedras

— DOC Boundaries
— Vinhos Regionais
Text in this style denotes Indicacao de Proveniencia Regulamentada (IPR)
Text in this style denotes Denominacao de Origem Controlada (DOC)
Text in this style denotes Vinhos Regional (VR)

Madeira
TERRAS
MADEIRENSES

Açores

Area Mapped
PORTUGAL   SPAIN

➢ PORTUGAL
  ▪ Portugal is adjacent to Spain as is known more for its ports than any other wine. Although they produce some great white wines from this regions. Most of the grapes are indigenous to Portugal. There are grapes used that come from other parts but mostly Portugal.
  ▪ An interesting note: The "term" is still used and made by other countries, unlike the term Champagne, Chablis, Burgundy, Sherry or even Tocai; The Port term or name has not been isolated to just Portugal. All other countries will use the same term. Eventually others may be forced to call a fortified wine made in the same tradition another name but for now port is port and as many as 80 different varietals are acceptable.
➢ Wine Laws"
  ▪ Vino da Mesa (VdT)
    • Basic Table Wine
  ▪ Vinho Regional (VR)
    • Regional Wine, the equivalent of Vin de Pays in France. Grapes that could come from anywhere within the Region.
  ▪ Indicação de Proveniência Regulamentada (IPR)
    • This is equivalent to the VDQS in France; a very small percentage of producers fall in this range.
  ▪ Denominação de Origem Controlada (DOC)
    • This level aligns with the AOC of France, taking on the highest rating for Portugal wines.
  ▪ Garrafeira
    • This refers move for label information, in this case that a red wine has been aged for at least 30 months including time in the bottle. White wine require a minimum of 12 months and all wines with a minimum of 11.5% alcohol.
  ▪ Reserva
    • Is a term used for the top quality wines of superior Vintage years. This does not occur every year.
  ▪ Instituto do Vinho da Madeira (IVM)
    • This agency regulates and manage the making of Madeira
  ▪ Instituto do Vinho do Porto (IVP)
    • This is the only agency that does not actually report to the IVV. The IVP is unique and completely supervises the selling of Port.
  ▪ Instituto da Vinha e Vinho (IVV)
    • This is the overall high order of Laws. Under the IVV (Institute of Viticulture and Wines).

➢ **Vinho Verde** is a region, a wine and style of wine. Verde typically refers to Green as a color but here green is use <u>only</u> in the sense of being young. Vinho Verde can be red or white, and in Portuguese's restaurant the term often refers simply to the younger wines on the wine list. The demarcated Vinho Verdes, however, come from north-west Portugal. Both red and white are strongly acidic, usually with a prickle of fizz, and are best drunk young and chilled with the local cuisine.
  ▪ Grapes Loureiro and Trajadura and (the Alvarinho grape)

- **Douro**
  - This region is named after the Douro River and produces wines of both port and table styles. There are over 80 varietals that can be used for port but the top varietals are:
  - Grapes:
    - Red: Touriga National, Tinto Roriz (the local name for Tempranillo)
    - White : Malvasia (white grape for port)
- **Bairrada**
  - Has for ages been the source of some of Portugal's best red table wine (though has recently been challenged by a new wave of reds from Port producers in the Douro. These can brim over with intense raspberry and blackberry fruit, though the tannin levels in some, take a few years to soften.
- **Dão**
  - Dao has steep slopes ideal for vineyards, a great grape growing climate for the local grape varieties. Yet it is only in the last decade that whites have been freshened up, and reds have begun to realize their expected potential.
- **Ribatejo**
  - Portugal's second largest wine region straddles the River Tagus (Tejo) upstream from Lisbon. Prolific vineyards on the fertile soils alongside the river are producing large volumes of increasingly good everyday reds.

- PORT STYLES:

- White – white grapes – off dry to sweet
  - Not readily available even though it is fairly simple and non complicated.
- Ruby – UK market – sweet – simple
  - This is the lesser of the red ports, in complexity and cost. There is little aging and use of lesser quality grapes.
- Reserve Ruby - better Ruby ports – age 5 years
  - Higher quality and longer aging
- Tawny – blending Ruby and White Ports
  - Typically there are two styles of Tawny port. Aged and un-aged (or young tawny). The young tawny is from lesser quality grapes with little to no aging.
  - Higher quality use of grapes and selection.
    - Tawny with an Indication of Age 5, 10, 15, 20, 25+
- Crusted British specialty (unfiltered)
  - The majority relegated to the UK. This is port un-filtered allowing a large amount of crusting to be present that offers interesting characteristics. A hearty port.
- Late Bottled Vintage (LBV) (undeclared year)
  - Port that is retained in the barrel until the very last minute and then bottled.
- Reserve Tawny
  - From a single harvest and aged a min of 8 years
- Colheita - Portugal – this is very rare
  - single vintage – min 8 years
- Vintage – Declared year – bottled when 2 years

➢ Single Quinta Vintage – Single Estates
  ▪ This is a high ranking vineyard estate
  ▪ Coming from a single year
  ▪ Typically isolated to a vineyard and not a year. Meaning the prominent vineyard did well despite not necessarily having a great year by the rest.

GRAPES OF GERMANY:

RED	WHITE
SPÄTBURGUNDER	RIESLING
DORNFELDER	SYLVANER
TROLLINGER	MÜLLER THURGAU
LEMBERGER	GEWÜRZTRAMINER
KERNER	RULANDER
	WEISSBURGUNDER
	SCHEUREBE

GERMANY: KEY APPELLATIONS DISCUSSED IN REGION:

GERMANY
- Mosel-Saar-Ruwer
- Ahr
- Baden
- Franken
- Hessische-Berstrasse
- Mittelrhein
- Nahe
- Pfalz
- Rheingau
- Rheinhessen
- Sachsen
- Saal-Unstrut

SOIL: Porous Slate, sand, loam.

CLIMATE: Coolest for growing grapes and most northern.

QUALITY CONTROLS AND LAWS:
- Tefelwein
- Landwein
- QbA
- QmP

* Komitee I. Gewachs (First Growth Committee)

The Laws provide four different levels for GERMANY and an interesting self impose quality control expectation.

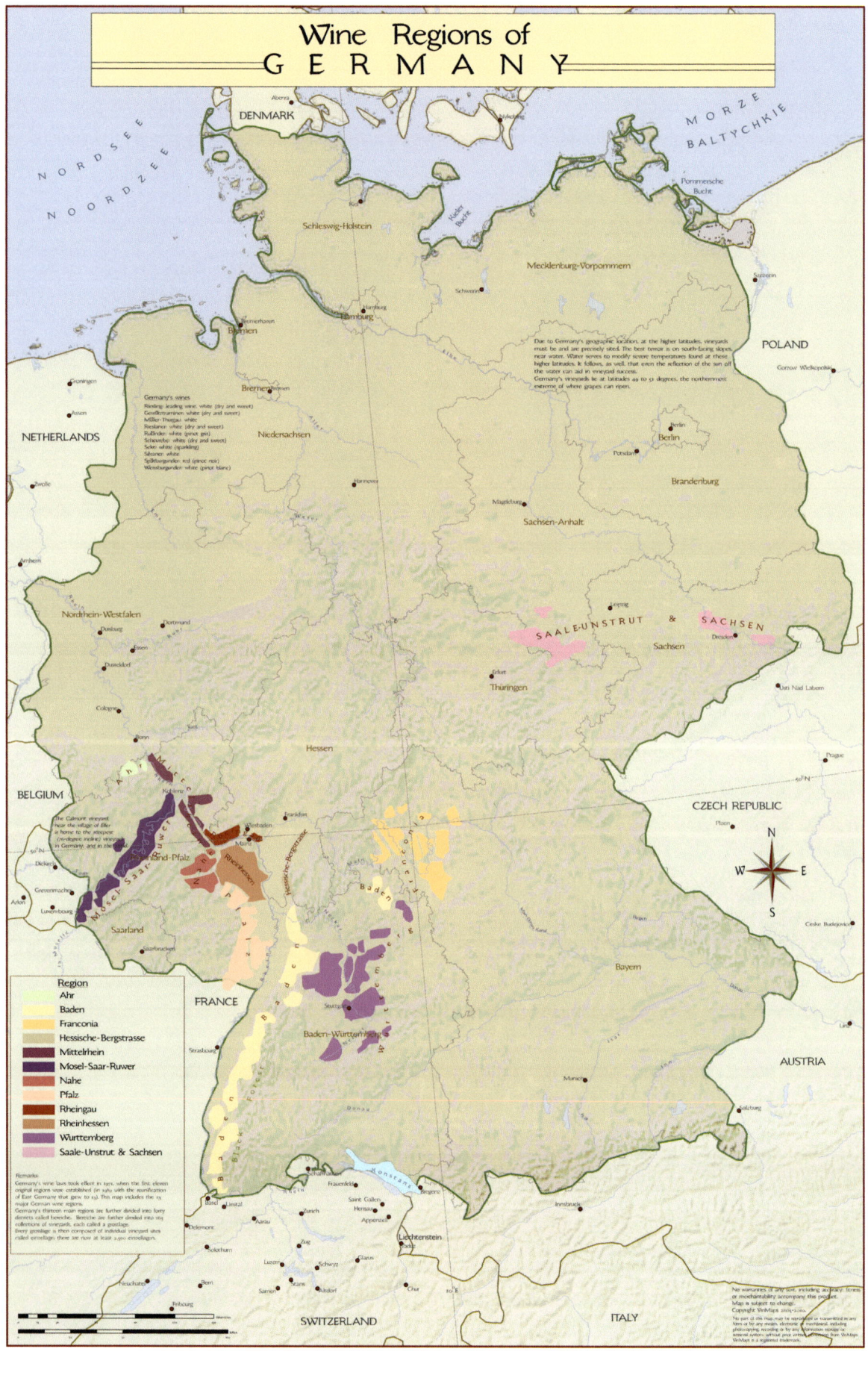

Wine Regions of
G E R M A N Y

Region
- Ahr
- Baden
- Franconia
- Hessische-Bergstrasse
- Mittelrhein
- Mosel-Saar-Ruwer
- Nahe
- Pfalz
- Rheingau
- Rheinhessen
- Wurttemberg
- Saale-Unstrut & Sachsen

Germany

This is about as far north as you can go and still grow grapes to make wine. As mentioned earlier, the grape growing zone falls between the 30th and 50th parallel north and south of the equator. Germany is just around the 50th parallel north of the equator.

German Wine Laws

- Germany will have two systems of classification for their wines and to complicate a bit more will have categories within those classification. One is based on the levels of sweetness and style, the other is based on their geographical classification.
- Let's take a look at the wine style based on sweetness first. On somewhat of the same order as France, we have level of quality in two categories the first two levels are very general without any real pedigree or much quality control.

- **Tafelwein**
  - This is the lowest level of the German wine classification, more accurately (Deutscher Tafelwein) in contrast to the Euro Tafelwein. German wines only contribute to less than 5% of this classification.
- **Landwein**
  - This is the next level up and was introduce in 1982 and is pretty much the equivalent of the Vin de Pays of France and as with Tafelwein, this classification represents less than 5% of the wine production.

- The next two categories are for Quality wines with greater pedigree and control.

  - **Qualitätswein bestimmter Anbaugebiet (QbA)**
    - This level applies more restrictions to the wine production. Wines in this classification must produce wines from one of the 13 Anbaugebiete. The use or blending of wines from other regions is strictly a "no no". The label must indicate the region, some indication of the style of the wine. This classification does allow the wines to be chaptalized, which will often have higher alcohol and / or sugar levels.
  - **Qualitätswein mit Prädikat (QmP)**
    - This classification is the highest of the German wine Laws. The grapes must come from a single Anbaugebiet and that name must appear on the label and from a single

Bereich. The wines of this classification can not chaptalised the must, meaning all natural sugars.
- "Komitee I. Gewachs (First Growth Committee)
  - This is still a self impose quality standard and effort. The intent is to address a higher standard of wine for the top growers.
    - o Riesling grape ONLY
    - o Hand harvest only
    - o Banning sweeteners (this exist already for QmP wines)
    - o Maximum yield of 3.2 tons per acre
    - o Minimum of 11% alcohol
    - o Minimum of 6 month aging before release
    - o Release two years after harvest
    - o Etc…
- Sparkling wine for Germany: Sekt is the term used for sparkling wine.
  - Grapes for Sekt are: Riesling, Rulander (Pinot Gris), and Weissburgunder (Pinot Blanc)

❖ Now to add a bit more complexity the QmP category offers styles and levels of sweetness at the (Must Level) and this is important, not at the wine level. Remember no Chaptalization and the following are the categories for a QmP.

❖ Note: these styles are base on (sugar level) at the Must stage.
- Kabinett
  - Light body and lower in sweetness.
- Spätlese
  - Meaning (Late Harvest). These wines are typically a bit heavier that Kabinett and a bit more sugar typically. Having said that, not all Spälese will be inherently sweeter, there is some overlap between each of the styles.
- Auslese
  - The next level up. These grapes are extra ripe and can range from a bit drier than some Spätlese to very sweet approaching the next level up if not a bit over.
- Beerenauslese (BA)
  - This next category continues the style with more selected grapes of full Botrytis ripeness. As mentioned earlier there are a few ways to obtain high degrees on sugar in the wine. Late Harvest which is typically the Kabinett and Spätlese, then to accomplish greater levels Botrytis in most case becomes necessary.
- Trockenbeerenauslese (TBA)
  - This category produces very low qualities of wine. Only the best vintages properly undergo the affects of Botrytis (shrivel to a raisin consistency). The water to sugar ratio, therefore reduces the production to a minimum. Once more the category of a TBA can vary with overlap to the different regions producing Beerenauslese to levels of much greater sweetness. TBA's can also vary from regions to region of their version of TBA.
- Eiswein (ice- wine)

- This wine is made from grapes that have been left on the vine to freeze during a climate situation where the temperature remains low and consistent for a period of time that cause the grapes to partially freeze (the more water content) and leaving the sugary flavor of the grape just below freezing. The grapes are harvested and press, extracting the juice and leaving the pressed frozen ice. The juice is then fermented accordingly. The level of sweetness for Eiswein can vary from drier that a TBA but in some cases can actually exceeding a TBA style.

The Geographical Classification

➢ **Anbaugebiet**
- This is a designated quality region. The vineyards of Germany are divided into 13 of these regions.

➢ **Bereich**
- This is a district within an Anbaugebiet (a quality region and may have several communes). To consider a bit more confusion, the higher levels of geographical classification can occur at multiple levels. An Einzellage or Grosslage can occupy at a Beriech level as well.

➢ **Gemeinde**
- This is a commune. This is equivalent to the term used in Burgundy France of "Village".

➢ **Grosslage**
- A group of adjoining Vineyards. This has been a downfall for a number of very high Einzellages because in 1971 when this law created the classification, it literally allowed some, maybe, many of the lesser vineyards to ride on the coattail of the more outstanding ones.

➢ **Einzellage**
- This is an individual vineyard. This is the highest level and the most important of the geographical classification. The dissatisfaction occurs by means of the information, not showing if the wine is an Einzellage or Grosslage, as in France, you have to commit to remember the more important and well know Einsellages. The price can be an indication but not one you can completely rely on.

As you can see, the geographical classification goes from a very general non-pedigree origin to a very specific and the most important vineyard.

Viticulture:

Vary considerably but for this effort, the most important will fall under the production of the QmP wines. Those vineyards are grown on steep slopes with full advantage of the river and river valleys. The water supports the moderating of temp and growing conditions. There are starting harvest dates the control with the actual harvest takes place.

Vinification:

Because of Germany located in the far north, the level of sugar development is extreme and may vary severely. In most cases, wines are chaptalised to compensate for the cooler temperatures preventing a full season of ripening development and obtaining the needed level of sugar to ensure alcohol levels. 75% of the grapes grown in Germany are just that, grown and then produced by others (co-operatives).

Grape Varietals for Germany

White	Red
Riesling	Spätburgunder
Gewurztraminer	Dornfelder
Müller Thurgau	Trollinger
Silvaner (Sylvaner)	Portugieser
Weissburgunder	Kerner
Scheurebe	Lemberger
Huxelrebe	
Ruländer	

❖ It is strongly recommended that you become familiar with a few of the key regions of Germany. All thirteen regions are listed but <u>a few are more notable than the others.</u>

➢ **Ahr**
  ▪ This is a small region along the river Ahr. The key note for this region is red wine production and Pinot Noir better known as Spätburgunder is responsible for that.
➢ **Baden**
  ▪ Baden is in the southwestern corner of Germany and just across from Alsace.
➢ **Franken**
  ▪ The only wine region situated in Bavaria.
➢ **Hessische Bergstrasse**
  ▪ This is a small region dominated by Riesling.
➢ **Mittelrhein**
  ▪ Located around the middle area of the river Rhine, primarily between the regions Rheingau and Mosel, and again the grape is by far, Riesling.
➢ **Mosel**
  ▪ This is the most important region and the one that commands the most attention. This is Riesling country but having said that, there really isn't a region in that Germany that doesn't grow some portion of Riesling. This area stretches along the *Mosel* River and its tributaries, the rivers Saar and Ruwer, and was previously known as *Mosel-Saar-Ruwer*. Eventually it was shorten to just Mosel. The key grape is most definitely Riesling. The wines are grown in on steep vineyards directly overlooking the rivers.
➢ **Nahe**
  ▪ Around the river Nahe; soil of volcanic origins.
➢ **Pfalz**
  ▪ The second largest producing region in Germany, Warmer than all other German wine regions. This region makes up the top 3, with the Mosel and Rheingau. Due to it being the warmest, it gives way to some of the best Botrytis style wines, Beerenauslese and Trockenbeerenauslese are products of that.
➢ **Rheingau**

- A small region situated on the bend of the river Rhine. The great region is in direct completion with the Mosel and does extremely well in the process. Again the leading grape is Riesling and reflects 80% of production.This is where the practice of the Prädikat originated. The oldest documented references to Riesling come from the Rheingau region.

> **Rheinhessen**
  - This region is the largest production area in Germany. Once known for Liebfraumilch (a very popular wine back in the United States around 1970's or there about, a soft wine of the inexpensive nature. Rheinhessen is the largest but only in production size, their best is under 10% from Riesling. The soil is more sandstone.

> **Saale-Unstrut**
  - One of regions in former East Germany along the rivers Saale and Unstrut, and Germany's northernmost wine growing region.

> **Sachsen**
  - The other region in former East Germany, in the southeastern corner of Germany.

> **Württemberg**
  - A traditional red wine region, Trollinger, the region's signature variety and Lemberger is another key varietal that does well here.

❖ There are 13 regions (*Anbaugebiete*)
❖ 39 districts (*Bereiche*)

GRAPES OF AUSTRIA:

RED	WHITE
PORTUGIESER	GRÜNER VELTLINER
BLAURER ZWEIGELT	MÜLLER THURGAU
SPÄTBURGUNDER	RIESLING

AUSTRIA: KEY APPELLATIONS DISCUSSED IN REGION:

AUSTRIA
Lower Austria
      (Niederösterreich)
Burgenland
Kamptal
Kemstal
Wachau

SOIL: Loess, Granite, Slate, Chalk, Loam and Gravel

CLIMATE: Very cold conditions, with warm summers.

QUALITY CONTROLS AND LAWS:

- Tafelwein (table wine),
- Qualitätswein (wine of quality)
- Prädikatswein ("certified" wine)

The Laws provide three different levels for AUSTRIA

AUSTRIA
Wine Regions

Brno

CESKÁ
REPUBLIKÁ

Kamptal
Kremstal
Wachau

Weinviertel

SLOVENSKÁ
REPUBLIKÁ

Traisental
Donauland
Wien
Vienna

Carnuntum

NIEDERÖSTERREICH
Thermenregion

Eisenstadt

Neusiedler
See

Neusiedlersee-Hugelland

BURGENLAND
Mittelburgenland
Südburgenland

Neusiedlersee

MAGYARORSZÁG
(HUNGARY)

Szombathely

STEIERMARK

Weststeiermark
Graz
Südoststeiermark

Südsteiermark

SLOVENIJA

N
W E
S

0   40   80 Kilometers

Austria

Austria

- **History**
  - New wine laws were most definitely needed and were introduced in 1993. At this point I do not wish to go over some of the misdoings and will let the student research some of these issues without the continuation of propagating a very difficult event that most would like to forget and focused on the outstanding quality controls and regulations that now are in place.
  - Most of Austria laws and wine making styles are much like Germany with the exception of possibly greater attention to quality.
  - Austrian wine law is based on European wine legislation
- ➤ **Wine laws (first enacted in 1972) based pretty much on Germany. Revamped in 1985**
  - Important elements of the label are origin, varietal, vintage, quality designation, alcohol content, residual sugar, official control number, producer, and bottler.
  - Austrian Qualitätswein and Prädikatswein are controlled twice by state laboratories: a chemical analysis is followed by a tasting commission. The official control number and the red-white-red band document this extensive process of control and quality assurance.
- ➤ **Viticulture**
  - Eastern half of Austria about 136,000 acres.
  - Climate: Mountainous nation warm summers and cold winters.
  - Soil: mostly Loess, granite, Chalk, Loam and gravel.
- ➤ **Wine regions**
  - Four wine growing regions
  - Lower Austria (Niederösterreich)
    - Kamptal (lower Austria)
    - Kremstal (dry whites)
    - Donauland (whites)
    - Carnuntum (from Vienna to the Slovakian border)
    - Wachau (Riesling) most planted
    - Austria's top region for dry whites
  - Burgenland (eastern border with Hungary) four wine regions
    - Neusiedler See (sweet wines)
      - This important wine growing region for red, dry white and dessert wines lies immediately to the north and east of the Neusiedler See itself.
    - Neusiedler See-Hügelland
      - Rich supple reds, fresh dry whites and dessert wines.
      - Rust
        - o One of Austria's most important wine towns (sweet wines)
    - Middle Burgenland
      - Blaufränkisch (robust)
    - South Burgenland

- ◆ Good reds and dry whites
  - Styria (in south- east Austria)
    - ◆ Full bodied white and un-oaked Chardonnay)
- ➢ Grapes (cold resistant and early ripening)
  - Gruner Veltliner (most widely planted)
  - Müller Thurgau (second most popular)
  - Reisling
  - Blaufrankisch
  - Portugieser
  - Zweigelt (developed by Dr. Zweigelt in 1922)
  - Welschriesling
  - Muscat (Muskateller)
  - St-Laurent
  - Gewurztraminer
  - Cabernet Sauvignon
- ➢ **Austrian wines**
  - Are mostly dry white wines primarily made from the Grüner Veltliner grape. The dessert wines have a great advantage due to Austrian's ability to produce the perfect climate of humidity, temperature and time duration for Botrytis (Noble Rot) to work at its best this is mostly around the region of Neusiedler See. About 30% of the wines are red, made from Blaufränkisch (also known as Lemberger).
- ➢ Austria is also home to the famous Riedel, makers of some of the most expensive wine and other stemware in the world.
  - There are 4 wine regions of Austria
    - (the underlined * regions are key regions to focus on)
  - **Lower Austria**
    - <u>Wachau</u> *
    - <u>Kremstal</u>*
    - <u>Kamptal</u>*
    - Traisental
    - Wagram (formerly Donauland)
    - Weinviertel
    - Carnuntum
    - Thermenregion
  - **Burgenland**
    - <u>Neusiedlersee</u>*
    - <u>Neusiedlersee- Hügelland</u>*
    - Mittelburgenland
    - Südburgenland
  - **Vienna**
    - Wien
  - **Styria**
    - Südoststeiermark
    - Südsteiermark
    - Weststeiermark

GRAPES OF ARFICA:

RED	WHITE
PINOTAGE	CHENIN BLANC
MERLOT	CHARDONNAY
SHIRAZ	SAUVIGNON BLANC
CABERNET SAUVIGNON	

AFRICA: KEY APPELLATIONS DISCUSSED IN REGION:

SOUTH AFRICA
- Constantia
- Overberg
- Paarl
- Robertson
- Stellenbosch
- Walker Bay
- Elgin

SOIL: Granite and Sandstone

CLIMATE: Moderated by the Atlantic

QUALITY CONTROLS AND LAWS:
- Wine of Origin (WO) under this are 4 Categories:
- Geographical Units
- Regional
- District
- Ward
  - Landwein wine-growers association.

The Laws provide four different levels for SOUTH AFRICA typically.

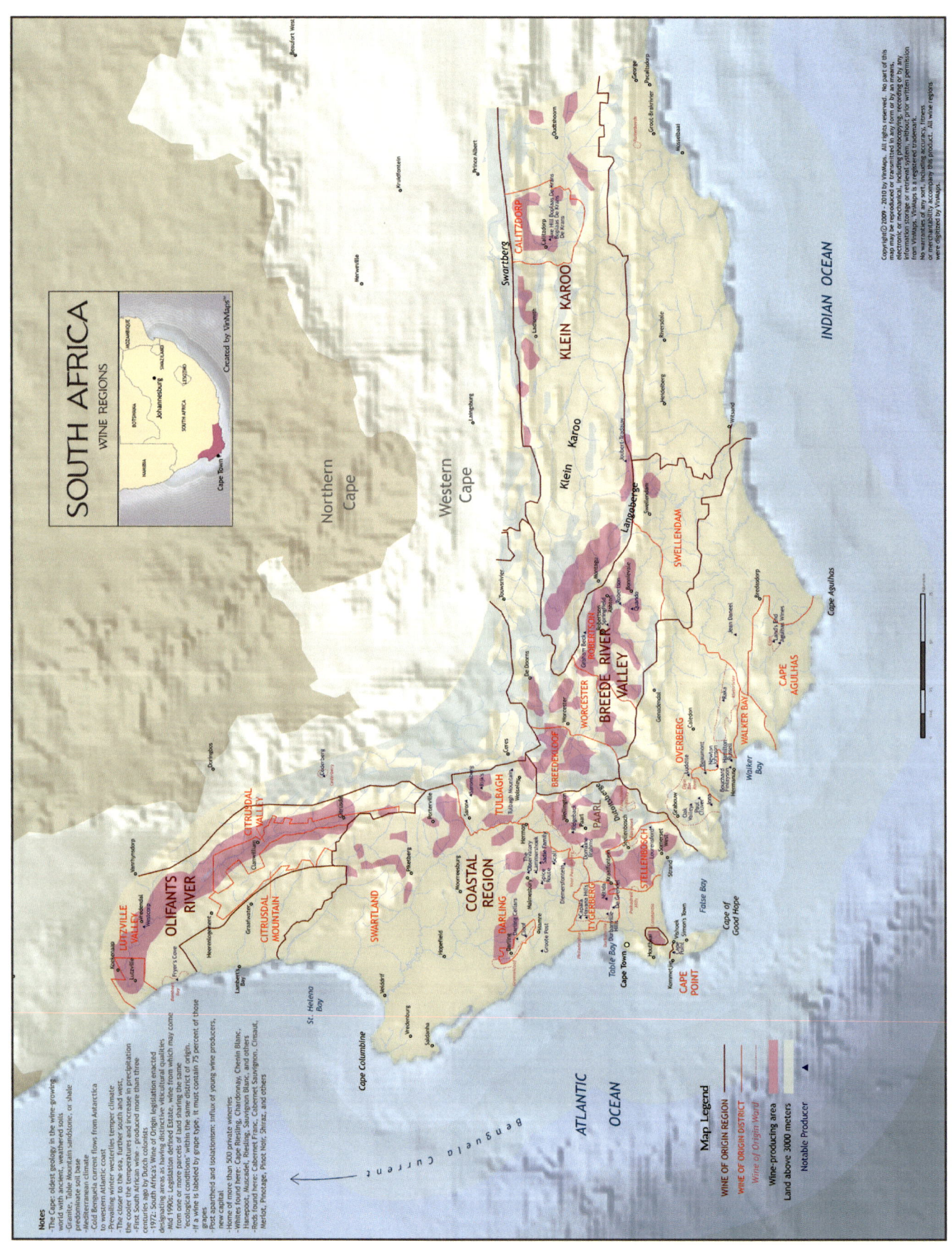

Notes

- The Cape: oldest geology in the wine-growing world with ancient, weathered soils
- Granite, Table Mountain sandstone, or shale predominate soil base
- Mediterranean climate
- Cold Benguela current flows from Antarctica to western Atlantic coast
- Prevailing winter westerlies temper climate
- The closer to the sea, further south and west, the cooler the temperatures and increase in precipitation
- First South African wine - produced more than three centuries ago by Dutch colonists
- 1972: South Africa's Wine of Origin legislation enacted designating areas as having distinctive viticultural qualities
- Mid 1990s: Legislation defined Estate wine from which may come from one or more parcels of land sharing the same 'ecological conditions' within the same district of origin.
- If a wine is labeled by grape type, it must contain 75 percent of those grapes.
- Post apartheid and isolationism: influx of young wine producers, new capital
- Home of more than 500 private wineries
- Whites found here: Cape Riesling, Chardonnay, Chenin Blanc, Hanepoot, Muscadel, Riesling, Sauvignon Blanc, and others
- Reds found here: Cabernet Franc, Cabernet Sauvignon, Cinsaut, Merlot, Pinotage, Pinot Noir, Shiraz, and others

SOUTH AFRICA
WINE REGIONS

Created by VinMaps™

Map Legend

—— WINE OF ORIGIN REGION

—— WINE OF ORIGIN DISTRICT

······ Wine of Origin Ward

▢ Wine-producing area

▢ Land above 3000 meters

▲ Notable Producer

South Africa

- ➤ Although there have been several locations in Africa that have attempted grape growing it turns out that only the southern end of the country has the best suited climate for grapes. Africa as a whole is a very hot region but as with other major wine growing regions, large bodies of water make it possible and probable in many cases to grow grapes suited for wine quality. In this case the moderating influences of the Indian Ocean to the south and breezes from the Atlantic Ocean to the west make this possible.
- ➤ Approximately 85% of all production is by co-operatives.
- ➤ The leading grape varietal is South Africa is Cabernet Sauvignon
- ➤ South Africa is of course New World but often show intentional characteristic of Old World wine styles.

- ➤ **Wine Laws and Regulations**
  - ▪ WO (WINE OF ORIGIN)
    - • The "wine of Origin" Controls or regulates how the wine regions of South Africa are defined. This is somewhat of a mixture of the AOC of France and of the AVA of North America. As with the AVA is regulates more of what goes on the label of the wine, than attempt to regulate: yield, varietal, alcohol percentage …etc.
- ➤ **The WO system has four categories.**
  - ▪ **Geographical Units:** example Western Cape
  - ▪ **Regions**: example Stellenbosch
  - ▪ **Districts**: example Walker Bay
  - ▪ **Wards**: example Elgin
    - • A "Ward" is the closest example of an area being defined by uniqueness of "Terrior".
- ➤ **Pinotage:** This is South Africa's flagship grape varietal. Originally set out to be the crossing of Pinot Noir and Syrah; Hence the name **Pinotage** (the front end of the word coming from Pinot Noir and the backend coming from the well known and respected region of Hermitage in southern France, known for Syrah. Later this flagship varietal was discovered to be the varietals of Pinot Noir and Cinsaut. After this discovery the name was left as is, without any further consideration of having the name reflect the now reveal varietal (both the Syrah and Cinsaut are Southern Rhone Varietals).
- ➤ **Pinotage**
  - ▪ Today it is the second most widely planted red grape variety in South Africa.

- This varietal is not planted anyway else in the world and therefore will struggle to become an internationally known varietal.
- The unique characteristic of this varietal conjured up reminiscence of Band-Aid which is not on the forefront of many.

➢ **Constantia**
- This is the heart of South Africa wines. It was divided into five areas, Groot Constantia, Klein Constantia and Buitenverwachting, Constantia Uitsig and Steenberg. Cape Town is where the first vineyards were planted in South Africa. The vineyards are planted on the slopes of Constantia Mountain.

➢ **Stellenbosch**
- Dramatic mountains are to be noted from a scenic view point and this is probably a good time to talk about pests that can plaque any given vineyard. The majority of time, vineyard managers contend with birds, dear, rodents, insects and of course extreme weather conditions. The Stellenbosch region faced a more unique issue, a major Baboon problem, quite intellectual and conning, they often manage to negotiate any perimeter deterrent erected. Towering mountains and many of the finest reds are associated with the region. Name after the University founded after Simons van der Stel 1679. It boasts the greatest concentration of wines in the Cape area. Just east of Cape Town, is Stellenbosch.
- There are several different sub-regions.
- Soil:
  - Granite-based in the east are suited for red wines,
  - Sandstone in the west is best for white wines.
- Stellenbosch is most noted for their premium red wines, Cabernets and Bordeaux blends.

➢ **Paarl**
- Paarl takes on a resemblance to the French Corner from a demographics stand point. Paarl accounts for nearly 19% of SA entire vineyard planting. This region is north-west of Cape Town and traditionally is considered a white wine region, but as of recent is now focusing more on reds. Paarl is typically hotter than Stellenbosch.
- Soil: Granite and Sandstone slate
- Climate: Wet winters and very hot summers.
- Grape:
  - The Palomino (key grape for Sherry in Jerez) can be as good as Spain sometime.

➢ **Overberg**
- Overberg is the Coolest area of SA located in the Western Cape
- Soil: Granite and Sandstone
- Climate: Mediterranean
- Grapes
  - Pinot Noir, Sauvignon Blanc.

➢ **Robertson**

- Robertson has more of an appearance of Australia, being more of horse country and Kangaroos. Robertson is east of Cape Town and is pretty much a hot region but surprisingly more noted for its white wines.
- Soil: Lime rich soils
- Climate: Hot dry inland area
- Grapes:
  - Reds: Shiraz and Cabernet Sauvignon
    - Shiraz also known and called Syrah is pronounced Shiraz in South Africa and Australia. The grape's origin is from a small town in Persia.
  - Whites: Chenin Blanc (aka Steen) and Colombard
    - Chardonnay and Muscat take a second position.

➢ **Elgin**
- Elgin is rather new to SA wine production with a cool-climate; east of Stellenbosch and more of a fruit growing area than wine production. The production of wine is dominated by Sauvignon Blanc and Pinot Noir. Having said that, Shiraz is expected to do well, keep in mind that this is a cool climate region.
- Soil: Clay based
- Climate: Atlantic Ocean influence
- Grapes:
  - White: Sauvignon Blanc
  - Red: Pinot Noir and Shiraz

➢ **Walker Bay**
- Walker Bay is another new and small cool-climate coastal wine region, south of Cape Town. About 12 or so wineries
- Soil: Clay
- Climate: Atlantic Ocean influence
- Grapes:
  - White: Chardonnay and Sauvignon Blanc
  - Red: Pinot Noir

GRAPES OF SOUTH AMERICA:

RED	WHITE
MERLOT	CHARDONNAY
CABERNET SAUVIGNON	SAUVIGNON BLANC
MALBEC	TORRONTES
CARMENÈRE	

SOUTH AMERICA: KEY APPELLATIONS DISCUSSED IN REGION:

SOUTH AMERICA

Chile
- Aconcagau
- Casablanca
- Maipo
- Central Valley
  - Rapel Valley
  - Curicó Valley
  - Maule Valley

Argentina
- Salta
- Mendoza
- Rio Negro

SOIL: Clay Loam and various

CLIMATE: Maritime mostly

QUALITY CONTROLS AND LAWS:
- See each region due to large variation

The Laws provide different levels and Traditions for SOUTH AMERICA

GRAPES OF CHILE:

RED	WHITE
CABERNET SAUVIGNON	CHARDONNAY
MERLOT	SAUVIGNON BLANC
PINOT NOIR	
CARMENÈRE	

SOUTH AMERICA: KEY APPELLATIONS DISCUSSED IN REGION:

CHILE
- Northern Chile
  - Aconcagua Valley
  - Casablanca Valley
- Central Chile
  - Maipo Valley
  - Rapel Valley
  - Curicó Valley
  - Maule Valley

SOIL: Alluvial mostly

Climate: Warm

QUALITY CONTROLS AND LAWS:
- No hard and fast laws
- Finas are varietal labeled
- Corrientes (ordinary wines)
- Reserva Especial (is used without much meaning) 85% varietal requirement

The Laws and Traditions of CHILE

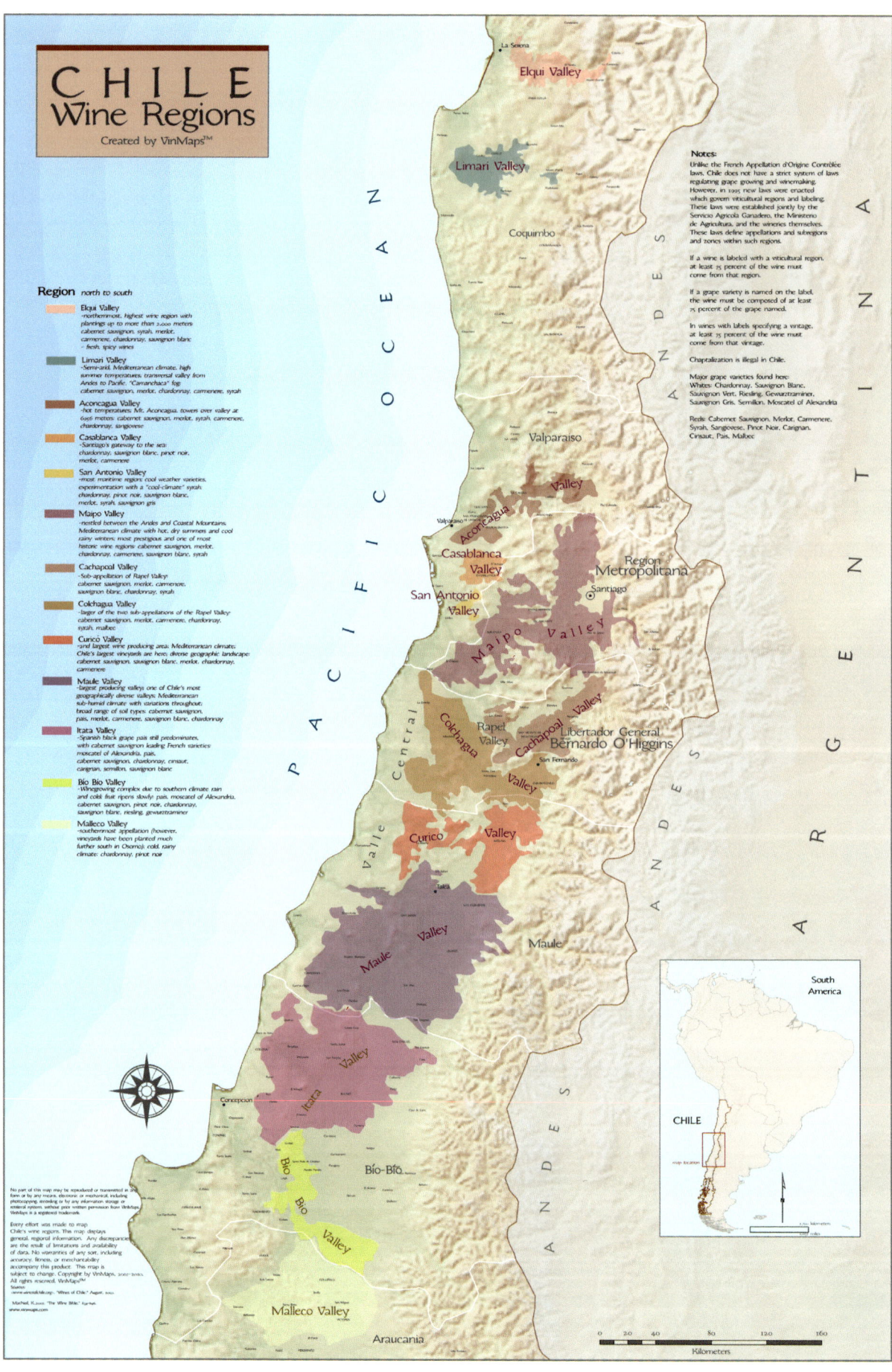

CHILE
Wine Regions
Created by VinMaps™

Region *north to south*

Elqui Valley
-northernmost, highest wine region with plantings up to more than 2,000 meters. cabernet sauvignon, syrah, merlot, carmenere, chardonnay, sauvignon blanc
- fresh, spicy wines

Limari Valley
-Semi-arid, Mediterranean climate, high summer temperatures, transversal valley from Andes to Pacific, "Camanchaca" fog. cabernet sauvignon, merlot, chardonnay, carmenere, syrah

Aconcagua Valley
-hot temperatures, Mt. Aconcagua towers over valley at 6,956 meters. cabernet sauvignon, merlot, syrah, carmenere, chardonnay, sangiovese

Casablanca Valley
-Santiago's gateway to the sea: chardonnay, sauvignon blanc, pinot noir, merlot, carmenere

San Antonio Valley
-most maritime region, cool weather varieties, experimentation with a "cool-climate" syrah, chardonnay, pinot noir, sauvignon blanc, merlot, syrah, sauvignon gris

Maipo Valley
-nestled between the Andes and Coastal Mountains. Mediterranean climate with hot, dry summers and cool rainy winters; most prestigious and one of most historic wine regions: cabernet sauvignon, merlot, chardonnay, carmenere, sauvignon blanc, syrah

Cachapoal Valley
-Sub-appellation of Rapel Valley: cabernet sauvignon, merlot, carmenere, sauvignon blanc, chardonnay, syrah

Colchagua Valley
-larger of the two sub-appellations of the Rapel Valley: cabernet sauvignon, merlot, carmenere, chardonnay, syrah, malbec

Curicó Valley
-2nd largest wine producing area. Mediterranean climate, Chile's largest vineyards are here, diverse geographic landscape: cabernet sauvignon, sauvignon blanc, merlot, chardonnay, carmenere

Maule Valley
-largest producing valley, one of Chile's most geographically diverse valleys. Mediterranean sub-humid climate with variations throughout: broad range of soil types: cabernet sauvignon, pais, merlot, carmenere, sauvignon blanc, chardonnay

Itata Valley
-Spanish black grape pais still predominates, with cabernet sauvignon leading French varieties. moscatel of Alexandria, pais, cabernet sauvignon, chardonnay, cinsaut, carignan, semillon, sauvignon blanc

Bío Bío Valley
-Winegrowing complex due to southern climate rain and cold, but fruit ripens slowly: pais, moscatel of Alexandria, cabernet sauvignon, pinot noir, chardonnay, sauvignon blanc, riesling, gewürztraminer

Malleco Valley
-southernmost appellation (however, vineyards have been planted much further south in Osorno); cold, rainy climate: chardonnay, pinot noir

Notes:
Unlike the French Appellation d'Origine Contrôlée laws, Chile does not have a strict system of laws regulating grape growing and winemaking. However, in 1995 new laws were enacted which govern viticultural regions and labeling. These laws were established jointly by the Servicio Agrícola Ganadero, the Ministerio de Agricultura, and the wineries themselves. These laws define appellations and subregions and zones within such regions.

If a wine is labeled with a viticultural region, at least 75 percent of the wine must come from that region.

If a grape variety is named on the label, the wine must be composed of at least 75 percent of the grape named.

In wines with labels specifying a vintage, at least 75 percent of the wine must come from that vintage.

Chaptalization is illegal in Chile.

Major grape varieties found here:
Whites: Chardonnay, Sauvignon Blanc, Sauvignon Vert, Riesling, Gewürztraminer, Sauvignon Gris, Semillon, Moscatel of Alexandria

Reds: Cabernet Sauvignon, Merlot, Carmenere, Syrah, Sangiovese, Pinot Noir, Carignan, Cinsaut, Pais, Malbec

PACIFIC OCEAN

ANDES

ARGENTINA

Elqui Valley

La Serena

Limari Valley

Coquimbo

Valparaiso

Aconcagua Valley

Casablanca Valley

San Antonio Valley

Region Metropolitana

Santiago

Maipo Valley

Colchagua Valley

Cachapoal Valley

Rapel Valley

Libertador General Bernardo O'Higgins

San Fernando

Curico Valley

Itata

Maule Valley

Maule

Valle Central

Itata Valley

Concepcion

Bío Bío Valley

Bío-Bío

Malleco Valley

Araucania

South America

CHILE

map location

0   20   40   80   120   160
Kilometers

South America

Chile

- Chile produces a number of international varietals.
- Carmenère is a major grape utilized extensively in Chile. Carmenère is the 6th Bordeaux varietal that no longer plays a major role in Bordeaux and a small role in parts of France.

- ❖ **NORTH-WEST CHILE**
  Aconcagau Region:
  There are two major sub-regions of Aconcagau, Aconcagau and Casablanca, with most of the emphasis around the town of Santiago.

- ➤ Aconcagau
  - Located in the northernmost region Chile and about 60 miles north of Santiago.
  - First grapes arrived by Maximiano Errazuriz in 1870
  - Robert Mondavi created a joint venture with Errazuriz in 1996
  - Grapes:
    - White: Chardonnay and Sauvignon
    - Red: Cabernet Sauvignon and Merlot and a rare amount of Carmenère
  - **Sub-region Aconcagau**
    - The sprawling Santiago suburbs are a continuous threat to much of the vineyard growth as the city expands but vineyards are doing surprising well. The most northern region of Chile is one the sub-region's Aconcagau Valley the climate is hot and dry chile's warmest region while moving closer to the coast is the other sub-region Casablanca Valley. Aconcagau Valley is primarily Cabernet Sauvignon and Merlot.
      - Cabernet Sauvignon, Merlot
  - **Sub-region Casablanca**
    - A cooler region offering Maritime weather and about 50 mile west of Santiago.
    - Concha Y Toro is noted for the first grape utilization for Casablanca.
    - Grapes:
      - Red: Pinot Noir
      - White: Chardonnay, sauvignon Blanc

❖ **CENTRAL VALLEY**
There are 4 major sub-regions within the central valley of Chile and this is Chile's largest viticultural region.

➢ Maipo Valley
  ▪ Chile's oldest wine region, which is divided into a number of sub-regions.
  ▪ The soil varies significantly in this region
  ▪ Grapes:
    • Red: Cabernet Sauvignon
➢ Rapel Valley
  ▪ One of Chile's most exciting regions due to the Carmenère varietal which in producing some outstanding wines these days. This grape lost much of its standing in Bordeaux when Phylloxera hit in the mid 1800's.
  ▪ Maritime weather
    • Grape: Carmenère (is the main event) and Merlot
➢ Curico Valley(125 south of Santiago) and is centered in the town of Curico.
  ▪ Soil: More clay loam and far more consistent than what is found just north in Maipo Valley.
  ▪ Grapes:
    • Red Cabernet Sauvignon, Merlot, Carmenère
    • Chardonnay, Sauvignon Blanc
➢ Maule Valley
  ▪ Maule Valley (Whites out number reds 2 to 1) but the Merlot does well in the clay soil.
  ▪ Maule is the largest area planted in Chile
  ▪ Grapes:
    • Red: Merlot
    • White: Chardonnay, Sauvignon Blanc

GRAPES OF ARGENTINA:

RED	WHITE
MALBEC	TORRONTÉS
CABERNET SAUVIGNON	CHARDONNAY
MERLOT	SAUVIGNON BLANC
PINOT NOIR	
TEMPRANILLO	

SOUTH AMERICA: KEY APPELLATIONS DISCUSSED IN REGION:

Argentina
- Salta
- Mendoza
- Rio Negro

SOIL: Alluvial mostly

Climate: Warm

QUALITY CONTROLS AND LAWS:
- Argentina's Instituto Nacional de Viniviticultura (INV)

The Laws and Traditions for Argentina

BOLIVIA

PARAGUAY

BRAZIL

URUGUAY

ARGENTINA
Wine Regions
Created by VinMaps®

Notes:

Wine exports and grape production are monitored by
Instituto Nacionale de Vitivinicultura. Unlike the French
Appellation d'Origine Côntrolée laws Argentina does not have
a strict system of laws regulating grape growing and winemaking.
However, there have been industry-led efforts to define specific
viticultural regions.

If a grape variety is named on the label, 80 percent of the wine
in a bottle must be produced from that grape.

Major grape varieties found here:

Whites: Chardonnay, Chenin Blanc, Criolla and Cereza,
Moscatel de Alejandria, Torrontes.

Reds: Barbera, Bonarda, Sangiovese, Tempranilla
(Spanish spelling of Tempranillo), Cabernet Sauvignon,
Malbec, Merlot.

Main wine regions are located in the west central part of the
country, along the foothills of the Andes Mountains-up to 4,000
feet above sea level. The climate here is mainly semidesert-like
with an average of 320 days of sunlight, and 8 to 10 inches of rainfall
per year. Irrigation is heavily employed yet vineyards are
mostly free of fungal diseases.

Mendoza is the most important region, followed by San Juan,
La Rioja, and Salta. About 60 percent of the total production of
fine wine is red. Sparkling wine is also important here.

Region

- Catamarca
  -Syrah
- Cordoba
- Jujuy
- La Pampa
- La Rioja
- Mendoza
  -malbec as well as cabernet sauvignon, merlot,
  tempranilla syrah, sangiovese
- Rio Negro
  -whites, sparkling wines
- Salta
  -torrontes, rustic versions of malbec
  and cabernet sauvignon highest vineyards
  at 1700 to 2300 meters above sea level
- San Juan
  -syrah
- Tucuman

Other:
Patagonia: Beginning to produce large
quantities of fine wines, reds and whites

PACIFIC OCEAN

CHILE

ANDES

PATAGONIA

ATLANTIC OCEAN

Jujuy
Salta
Tucuman
Catamarca
La Rioja
San Juan
Mendoza
Rio Negro
Neuquen
Chubut
Santa Cruz
Tierra del Fuego

Formosa
Chaco
Corrientes
Misiones
Santiago del Estero
Santa Fe
Entre Rios
Cordoba
San Luis
Buenos Aires
Distrito Federal
Buenos Aires
La Pampa
PAMPAS

Gulf of
San Matías
Peninsula Valdés
Gulf of San Jorge
Cape Tres Puntas

Cape
San Antonio

Falkland Islands

South
America

ARGENTINA

Map
Location

Kilometers
0   80   160   320   480

Kilometers

Argentina

- Very big on exports, Argentina ranks 5th in wine production in the world.
- Malbec is the major grape varietal in Argentina. Malbec remains a minor grape varietal for the blend of Bordeaux and continue on the down fall of use. On the other hand, it gains greater and greater recognition in Argentina.
- Torrontés is the other key grape, a white varietal producing some very fresh and aromatic wines in Argentina especially in the Northern region of Salta.

➢ Wine Laws
  - Argentina's Instituto Nacional de Viniviticultura (INV)
    • Much like the AOC or DOC of France and Italy respectively, regulated, the pruning methods, harvesting, transporting of grapes, release dates, and Minimum and Maximum alcohol percentages.

➢ Salta
  - Salta was the first step for Argentina's role in grape growing, extending as far back as the mid 1500's.
  - Grape:
    • Red: Criolla
    • White: Torrontés

➢ Mendoza
  - Mendoza accounts for 75% of all vines planted in the region. Located in the western part of the region, the vineyards extend from sea level to roughly 4000 feet. Much of it is bulk type wines but a noticeable amount is premium wines.
  - Grapes:
    • Red: Malbec, Cabernet Sauvignon, and Tempranillo
    • White: Chardonnay

➢ Rio Negro
  - Rio Negro is giving some attention as it is responsible for 10% of Argentina's wine production. Somewhat of a warmer region reds are the dominating grape.

GRAPES OF AUSTRALIA:

RED	WHITE
CABERNET SAUVIGNON	CHARDONNAY
SHIRAZ	RIESLING
MERLOT	MUSCAT
	SÉMILLON

AUSTRALIA: KEY APPELLATIONS DISCUSSED IN REGION:

AUSTRALIA
- South Australia
  - Clare Valley
  - Barossa Valley
  - Eden Valley
  - Adelaide Hills
  - McLaren Vale
  - Padthaway
  - Coonawarra
- New South Wales
  - Mudgee
  - Hunter Valley
- Victoria
  - Rutherglen
  - Bendigo
  - Yarra Valley
- Western Australia
  - Margaret River

SOIL: Various

CLIMATE: Moderate to Continental

QUALITY CONTROLS AND LAWS:
- Geographical Indication (GI)

The Laws providing Regulation and Identification for AUSTRALIA

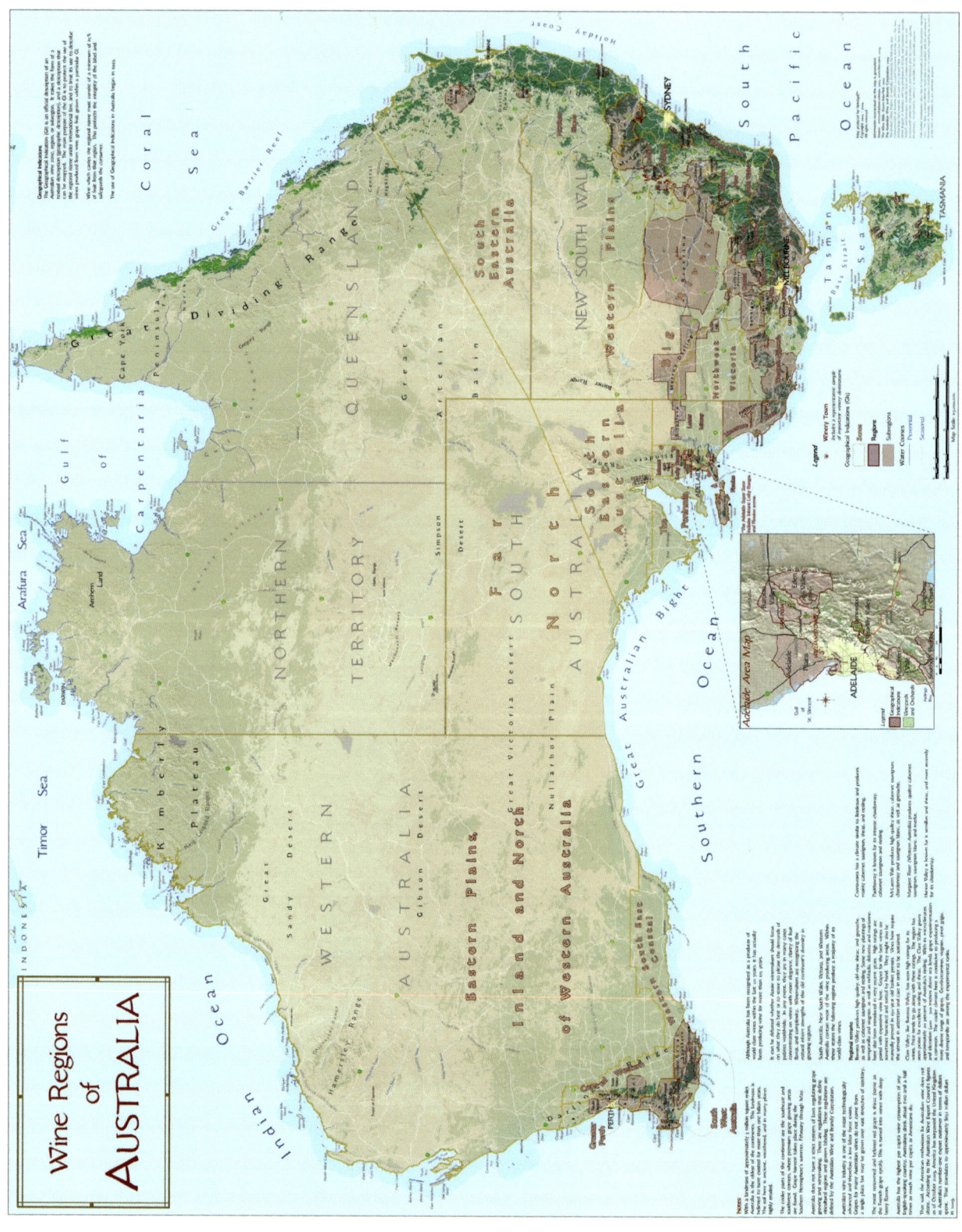

Wine Regions
of
AUSTRALIA

Australia

❖ Wine Laws and Quality Control

➤ **Geographic Indications**
  ▪ A Geographical Indication (GI) is an official description of an Australian wine zone, region or sub-region. It takes the form of a textual description (i.e. a list of grid references, map coordinates, roads and natural landmarks which can be traced to outline the regional boundary) along with a map. Its main purpose is to protect the use of the regional name under international law, limiting its use to describe wines produced from wine grape fruit grown within that GI.
  ▪ A Geographic Indication can be likened to the Appellation naming system used in Europe (e.g. Bordeaux, Burgundy) but is much less restrictive in terms of viticultural and winemaking practices. In fact the only restriction is that wine which carries the regional name must consist of a minimum of 85% of fruit from that region. This protects the integrity of the label and safeguards the consumer.
➤ **States and territories: 8**
  ▪ South Eastern Australia Zone (covers the eastern seaboard of Australia taking in parts of Queensland, NSW, Victoria and Tasmania)
  ▪ Wine Zones: 29
  ▪ Wine Regions: 62 (registered)
  ▪ Wine Sub-regions: 10 (registered
➤ The Dominant Grape are:
  ▪ Red: Shiraz followed by Cabernet Sauvignon
  ▪ White: Chardonnay
➤ Chaptalization is illegal but acidification is acceptable.

"The States, Territories, Zones, Regions and sub-regions listed are a shorter version. Again, the attempt is to identify the Key areas for most exams for wine courses".

❖ **South Australia (SA)**
  ➤ **There are: 7 Wine Zones: and 1 Superzones: Wine Regions: 17 Wine Sub-regions: 3**
  ➤ **Not all are listed.**

➢ Is divided into "Zones" but again in keeping with the intent of this text we will limit our coverage.

❖ **Adelaide Super Zone**
- (Sauvignon Blanc; Chardonnay; and Pinot Noir)
- Exist primarily to allow wineries of blended wines from any of the regions or zones within its boundary to use a single GI.
- The Adelaide Super-Zone is the official umbrella term for the Mt. Lofty Ranges Zone, Barossa Zone and the Fleurieu Zone. It contains many of Australia's most famous wine regions.
- They are united by their proximity to the broken run of the Mt. Lofty Ranges from Kangaroo Island through to the state's mid-north past the Clare Valley.
- However, the climate is very diverse; from the cold, windswept Kangaroo Island and the frosty Adelaide Hills to the baking Adelaide Plains

❖ **Barossa Zone**
➢ **Barossa Valley**
- Adelaide is the Capital.
- Now have 6th generation winegrowing families and blocks of vines over 150 years old. Adjoining Eden Valley. Also noted for Port style wines
- Climate: Warm and dry with low humidity and rainfall. It is Continental in nature. Cool & Cold nights and hot summers.
- Soil and Topography: Sub Valleys and twisting hills result in varying slopes; aspects and sites.
- Principal grapes
  - White: Semillon; Chardonnay; Riesling
  - Red: Shiraz; Cabernet Sauvignon; Merlot; Grenache; and Mourvèdre
➢ **Eden Valley**
- Background: First vines planted in 1847 by Cap. Joseph Gilbert.
- Climate: Cool and windswept; Much cooler than Barossa.
- Soil and Topography: around 1500 ft. From loamy sand to clay loam. Ironstone and Quartz gravels.
- Principal Grapes:
  - White: Riesling; Chardonnay
  - Red: Shiraz; Cabernet Sauvignon; Merlot

❖ **Mount Lofty Ranges Zone**
➢ **Adelaide Hills**
- Background Small and exciting region; about 30 min from Adelaide.
- Climate: Cool
- Soil and Topography: high altitude; loamy sands and clay
- Principal Grapes:
  - White: Chardonnay; Sauvignon Blanc
  - Red: Pinot Noir; Cabernet Sauvignon; Merlot; Shiraz

- ➢ **Clare Valley**
  - ▪ Background: Approximately 60% annual rainfall between May and September.
  - ▪ Valley north of Adelaide
  - ▪ Climate: Deceptively moderate climate
  - ▪ Soil and Topography: Significant limestone
  - ▪ Principal Grapes:
    - • White: Riesling; Chardonnay; Semillon; Sauvignon Blanc
    - • Red: Shiraz; Cabernet Sauvignon; Merlot; Malbec; Grenache
- ➢ **Adelaide Plains** (runs north of the city of Adelaide)
  - ▪ Background: source of low cost grapes. Joe Grilli probably most noted.
  - ▪ Climate: Hot and very hot!
  - ▪ Soil and Topography: laser flat; red-brown loamy sand and limestone and deeper levels.
  - ▪ Principal Grapes:
    - • White: Chardonnay; Colombard
    - • Red: Shiraz; Cabernet Sauvignon; Grenache; Merlot

- ❖ **Fleurieu Zone**
  - ➢ **McLaren Vale**
    - ▪ Background: About 45 small wineries; once a port area, nowadays it is good for full-bodied whites and reds.
    - ▪ Climate: Warm, sunny Maritime; Substantial meso-climate
    - ▪ Soil and Topography: Sandy Loam
    - ▪ Principal Grapes:
      - • White: Chardonnay; Semillon; Sauvignon Blanc; Riesling; Chenin Blanc
      - • Red: Shiraz; Cabernet Sauvignon; Grenache; Merlot; Pinot Noir; Cabernet Franc; Petit Verdot
  - ➢ **Langhorne Creek (Alfred Langhorne 1841)**
    - ▪ Background: Rapid recent growth; historically, grapes were trucked out to clients in Barossa and McLaren Vale. The oldest winery is the nostalgic Bleasdale. Irrigation is afforded by regular flooding of the Bremer River.
    - ▪ Climate: occasionally hot weather.
    - ▪ Soil and Topography: deep alluvial soil
    - ▪ Principal Grapes:
      - • White: Chardonnay; Riesling; Verdelho
      - • Red: Cabernet Sauvignon; Shiraz; Merlot;; Grenache

- ❖ **Limestone Coast Zone**
  - ▪ The ancient coastal dunes and seabed formations which give the Limestone Coast its name. Technically known as non-cracking subplastic clays.
  - ➢ **Coonawarra**
    - ▪ Background: This small patch of land can produce sublime Cabernets. An exporting led to planting boom of hundreds of acres. Holds the position as Australia's greatest Cabernet Sauvignon wine region. 1890 to 1945 major failures occurred

- Climate: This was the first cool-climate viticultural region to gain national prominence. Due to the limited maritime influence, the winters are cold, wet and windy.
- Soil and Topography: Terra Rossa Soil; Coonawarra boasts the most celebrated vineyard soil in Australia. Commonly known as "Terra Rossa". A distinctive, albeit thin, band of … at times vivid red soil.
- Principal Grapes:
  - White: Chardonnay; Riesling Semillon; Sauvignon Blanc
  - Red: Cabernet Sauvignon; Shiraz; Merlot; Pinot Noir; Cabernet Franc

➢ **Padthaway**
- Background: A lack of wineries makes this large vineyard area a tourist non-event. This area is the alter-ego of Coonawarra, growing whites to complement Coonawarra's Reds. Once thought to be a very upcoming and promising wine region. It was not until 1998 that major players became active. Padthaway falls within a buffer zone between Victoria and South Australia which imposes strict controls on water usage with no further irrigation rights being granted
- Climate
- Soil and Topography
- Principal Grapes:
  - White: Chardonnay; Riesling Semillon; Gewürztraminer; Sauvignon Blanc; Verdelho
  - Red: Shiraz; Cabernet Sauvignon; Merlot; Pinot Noir; Malbec

➢ **Mount Benson**
- Background: Fairly new region of planting along the coast, 1989. Vast underground water table. The famous Rhone Valley firm Chapoutier some importance on the area when it went in on a joint venture of 38 hectare biodynamic vineyard
- Climate: Maritime; cool; ocean one side / Robe lakes the other side.
- Soil and Topography: Terra Rossa; Limestone
- Principal Grapes:
  - White: Chardonnay; Sauvignon Blanc; Semillon
  - Red: Shiraz; Merlot; Pinot Noir

➢ **Wrattonbully** (Koppamurra)
- Background: Another GI issue. The winery Koppamurra was the dominate factor here and it would have made sense to GI the area as Koppamurra but instead Wrattonbully won out. "Tapanappa" note…
- Climate: The climate falls between that of Coonawarra and Padthaway. Warmer the Coonawarra but cooler that Padthaway. High humidity and rail fall making this high risk.
- Soil and Topography: Undulating slopes 75 to 300 ft. asl and planted in Terra Rosa, deriving from ancient coastal dunes.
- Principal Grapes:
  - White: Chardonnay
  - Red: Cabernet Sauvignon; Shiraz; Merlot

❖ **Lower Murray Zone**

- ➢ **Riverland**
  - ▪ Background: A vast irrigated region of 3 states; Victoria, South Australia and New South Wales… along the Murray River producing about 27% of the nations grapes, about 55% of South Australia This area has mainly given way to bulk and cheaper bottles of table wine and fortified wine. But now showing higher signs of quality as well.
  - ▪ Climate: hot and low rainfall; irrigation essential
  - ▪ Soil and Topography: red / brown sandy loam
  - ▪ Principal Grapes:
    - • White: Chardonnay; Muscat Gordo Blanco; Colombard
    - • Red: Cabernet Sauvignon; Grenache; Merlot; Petit Verdot

- ❖ **New South Wales**
  - ▪ New South Wales (NSW)
  - ▪ There are: 8 Wine Zones: Wine Regions: 16 (Murray Darling & Swan Hill cross into Victoria) Wine Sub-regions: 1
  - ➢ **Not all are listed.**

- ❖ **Hunter Zone**
  - ➢ **Hunter Valley (Chardonnay is the main stay)**
  - ➢ **Upper Hunter Valley**
    - ▪ Background
    - ▪ Climate
    - ▪ Soil and Topography
    - ▪ Principal Grapes:
      - • White: Chardonnay; Semillon
      - • Red: Shiraz; Cabernet Sauvignon
  - ➢ **Lower Hunter Valley**
    - ▪ Lower Hunter Valley
    - ▪ Background
    - ▪ Region
    - ▪ Climate
    - ▪ Soil and Topography
    - ▪ Principal Grapes:
      - • White: Semillon; Chardonnay; Verdello
      - • Red: Shiraz; Cabernet Sauvignon

- ❖ **Central Ranges Zone**
  - ➢ **Mudgee**
    - ▪ Background
    - ▪ Climate
    - ▪ Soil and Topography
    - ▪ Principal Grapes:
      - • White: Chardonnay; Semillon

- Red: Cabernet Sauvignon; Shiraz; Sangiovese; Barbera and Nebbiolo
- ➢ **Victoria (VIC)**
  - ▪ **Wine Zones: 6 Wine Regions: 20 (Murray Darling & Swan Hill cross into NSW) Wine Sub-regions:1**
  - ▪ More densely populated than that of any other state. More regions and more wineries than South Australia.
- ➢ **Port Phillip Zone** (Spectacular scenery)
  - ▪ Background:
  - ▪ Climate: cool Mediterranean
  - ▪ Soil and Topography
  - ▪ Principal Grapes:
    - • White: Chardonnay; Muscat Gordo Blanco; Colombard
    - • Red: Cabernet Sauvignon; Grenache; Merlot; Petit Verdot
- ➢ **Yarra Valley**
  - ▪ Background: dates back to 1838 for grape growing
  - ▪ Climate: Cool
  - ▪ Soil and Topography: hillside; sandstone; volcanic
  - ▪ Principal Grapes:
    - • White: Chardonnay; Sauvignon Blanc
    - • Red:; Pinot Noir; Cabernet Sauvignon; Shiraz; Merlot

- ❖ **Central Victoria Zone**
  - ➢ **Bendigo**
    - ▪ Background: (which came first wine or gold)? 1851 discovery of gold and by 1864 there were more than 40 vineyards in the Bendigo region. By 1880 over 100 wineries. Phylloxera in 1893… ended all. A gap of 60 years followed.
    - ▪ Climate: Strongly Continental
    - ▪ Soil and Topography: Sand; stony clay; lime; gypsum
    - ▪ Principal Grapes:
      - • White: Sauvignon Blanc; Chardonnay
      - • Red: Shiraz; Cabernet Sauvignon; Merlot
  - ➢ **Goulburn Valley & Nagambie Lakes**
    - ▪ Background: Phylloxera again taking its toll. High – stakes gambling; initial failure; glory and premature death and overnight success.
    - ▪ Climate: Warm region; moderate rainfall
    - ▪ Soil and Topography: red / brown sandy loam
    - ▪ Principal Grapes:
      - • White: Chardonnay; Sauvignon Blanc; Marsanne
      - • Red: Shiraz; Cabernet Sauvignon; Merlot

- ❖ **North East Victoria Zone**
  - ➢ **Rutherglen**
    - ▪ Background
    - ▪ Climate

- Soil and Topography
- Principal Grapes:
  - White: Muscadelle; Chardonnay; Marsanne
  - Red: Shiraz; Cabernet Sauvignon; Durif; Brown Muscat a Petits Grains
- ➢ **Western Australia (WA)**
  - **There are: 5 Wine Zones: Wine Regions: 9 Wine Sub-regions: 6**
- ➢ **Not all are listed.**
- ➢ **Margaret River**
  - Background
  - Climate: Maritime with the lowest average temp and Mediterranean climate in terms of rainfall.
  - Soil and Topography: Gravelly, sandy loam, granite.
  - Principal Grapes:
    - White: Chardonnay, Sauvignon Blanc, Chenin Blanc, Verdelho
    - Red: Shiraz; Cabernet Sauvignon, Merlot

Greater listing of Australia's Wine Region

- ➢ South Australia
  - Clare Valley
  - Barossa Valley
  - Eden Valley
  - Adelaide Hills
  - McLaren Vale
  - Padthaway
  - Coonawarra
- ➢ New South Wales
  - Mudgee
  - Hunter Valley
  - Riverina
- ➢ Victoria
  - Murray Darling
  - Rutherglen
  - Glenrowan
  - Goulburn Valley
  - Bendigo
  - Pyrenees
  - Macedon
  - Grampiana
  - Yarra Valley
  - Geelong
  - Mornington Peninsula
- ➢ Western Australia
  - Swan Valley

- Perth Hills
- Margaret River
- Great Southern Region
- Pemberton

GRAPES OF NEW ZEALAND:

RED	WHITE
PINOT NOIR*	SAUVIGNON BLANC*
CABERNET SAUVIGNON	CHARDONNAY
SYRAH	SÉMILLON
MERLOT	PINOT GRIS

*key grapes

NEW ZEALAND:
KEY APPELLATIONS
DISCUSSED IN REGION:

NEW ZEALAND
North Island
    Gisborne
    Hawke's Bay
South Island
    Marlborough
    Central Otago

SOIL: Various; much of Clay and Loam type.

CLIMATE: Mild in general

Exception: Central Otago Continental.

QUALITY CONTROLS AND LAWS:
- The Food regulation of 1984
- Trans – Tasman (replacing the previous)
- The Geographical Indication Act 1994 (GI)
- New revision is currently underway

The Laws and Regulations provide wine making controls for NEW ZEALAND

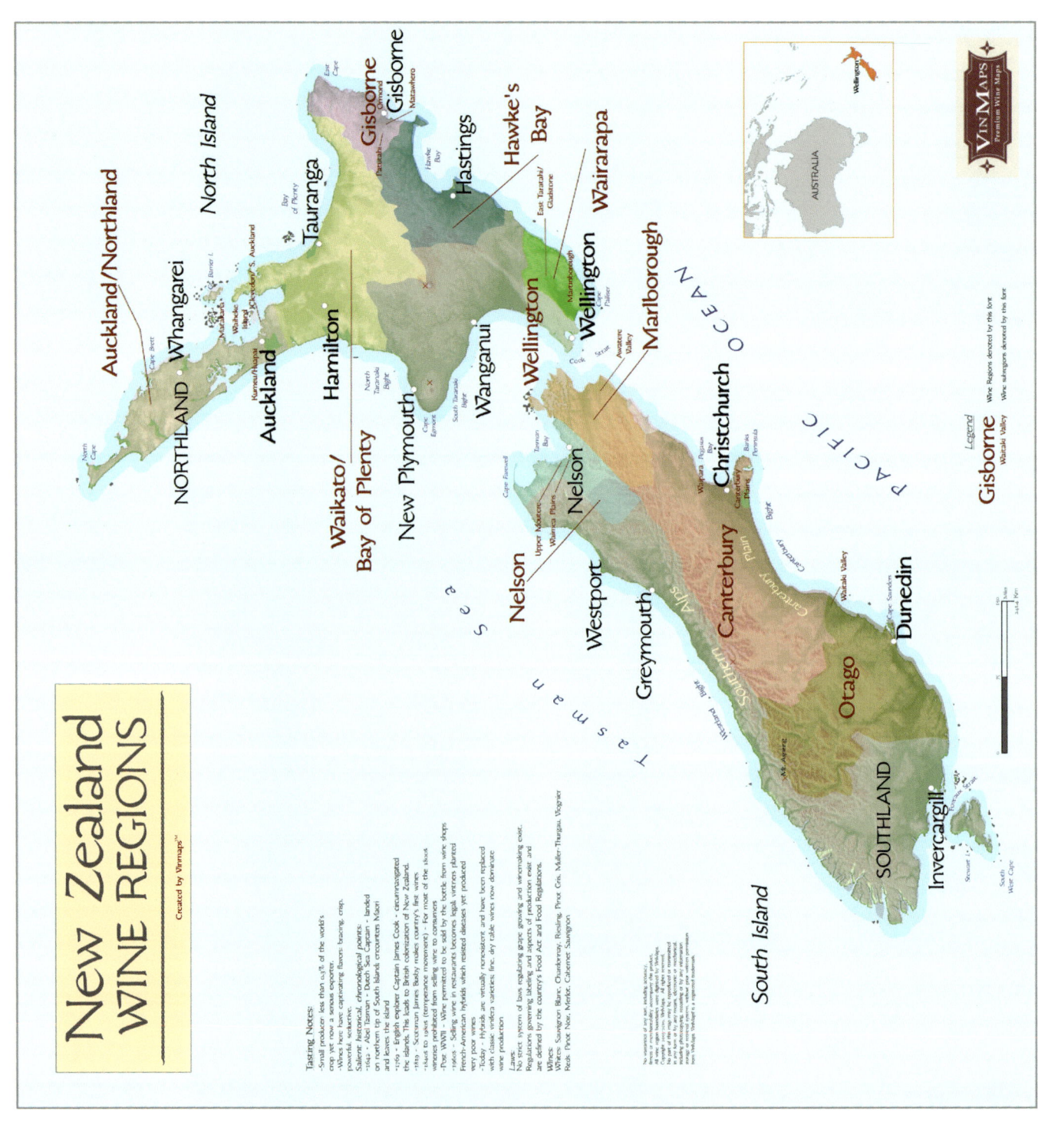

New Zealand
WINE REGIONS

Created by Vinmaps™

Tasting Notes:

-Small producer less than 0.5% of the world's crop yet now a serious exporter

-Wines here have captivating flavors: bracing, crisp, powerful, seductive.

Salient historical, chronological points:

-1642 – Abel Tasman – Dutch Sea Captain – landed on northern tip of South Islands encounters Maori and leaves the island

-1769 – English explorer Captain James Cook – circumnavigated the islands. This leads to British colonization of New Zealand.

-1819 – Reverend James Busby makes country's first wines

-1840s to 1960s (temperance movement) – For most of the 1800s wineries prohibited from selling wine to consumers

-Post WWII – Wine permitted to be sold by the bottle from wine shops

-1960s – Selling wine in restaurants becomes legal, vintners planted French-American hybrids which resisted diseases yet produced very poor wines

-Today – Hybrids are virtually nonexistent and have been replaced with classic vinifera varieties. Fine, dry noble wines now dominate wine production.

Laws:

No strict system of laws regulating grape growing and winemaking exist. Regulations governing labeling and aspects of production exist and are defined by the country's Food Act and Food Regulations.

Wines:

Whites: Sauvignon Blanc, Chardonnay, Riesling, Pinot Gris, Müller-Thurgau, Viognier

Reds: Pinot Noir, Merlot, Cabernet Sauvignon

North Island

Auckland/Northland
Whangarei
NORTHLAND • Auckland
Tauranga
Hamilton
Waikato/ Bay of Plenty
New Plymouth
Wanganui
Gisborne
Hastings
Hawke's Bay
Wairarapa
Wellington
Marlborough
Nelson
Westport
Greymouth
Christchurch
Canterbury
Otago
Dunedin
SOUTHLAND
Invercargill
South Island

PACIFIC OCEAN

Tasman Sea

AUSTRALIA

VinMaps
Premium Wine Maps

Legend

Gisborne — Wine Regions denoted by this font
Waitaki Valley — Wine subregions denoted by this font

New Zealand

- New Zealand is divided (grown) into two island, north and south and boast some of the newest land mass in the world from a geological stand point, hosting a variety of rocks and landforms with a great deal of clay and loam soils. Heavy rainfalls and humidity are standard. Croatian are very much responsible for a great deal of the grape growing / wine making history and background.
- Sauvignon Blanc is probably the first thing to come to mind when the subject of New Zealand comes up, maybe second to the Kiwi. But Sauvignon Blanc is what New Zealand is known for and what they really hang the hat on. It is the flagship varietal for this area, even though the country is quite capable of producing a number of other varietal with rather high standards and consistency.
- In the spirit of the textbook, four of the top 10 wine producing areas of New Zealand were chosen because of the high visibility of the regions as far as their overall appeal and production rate. Of the four listed below, Marlborough and Hawke's Bay lead the pack.
- Wine Laws:
  - There has been a number of established laws and guidelines supporting the effort for better quality and control of wine produced in New Zealand. The Food and Drug Act, later the Food Regulations of 1984, with revision in 2002 and current undertakings. The Geographical Indication Act of 1994 was much of the same with Australia, not controlling any of the aspects that an AOC would address but more or less some labeling controls on the boundary definition, regional government areas. This also looks much like the AVA of the United States.

- North Island
  - **Gisborne**
    - Gisborne is responsible for nearly 25% of the wine produced in New Zealand. It is located about two thirds down on the north Island. Gisborne experiences typical early harvest due to early rainfall and the attempt to prevent disease and grape rot.
    - Chardonnay is the more renowned grape but Gewurztraminer is a definite second, if not equal, in terms of show appeal. Botrytis can occur by definition of (warm weather and humidity in early morning to afternoon).
    - Soil: Alluvial loams
    - Grapes:
      - Red: Pinot Noir, Merlot

- White: Chardonnay, Muscat, Semillon, Müller Thurgau
  - **Hawke's Bay**
    - Hawke's bay is definitely the attention getter. Chardonnay and Merlot are the two key varietals that dominate this part of the region.
    - Soil: Diverse with Silty loams as the key soil type.
    - Grapes:
      - Red: Merlot, Cabernet Sauvignon, Pinot Noir, Cabernet Franc
      - White: Chardonnay, Sauvignon Blanc

- South Island
  - **Marlborough**
    - The north-eastern region of the south island is home to some of the most notable Sauvignon Blanc in the world. You just can't miss that signature style of herbaceous aromas of freshly mowed lawn, green apple and flinty character that Marlborough Sauvignon Blanc has become most famous for. The coolness of the region plays a great role for not only the Sauvignon Blanc but for Riesling and Gewurztraminer as well. There is some Pinot Noir grown there with much success for red. The other red varietal do not thrive as well.
    - Cloudy Bay certainly gets a fair amount of credit as one of the top produces for Sauvignon Blanc and other white varietals.
    - Soil: Various
    - Grapes:
      - Red: Pinot Noir
      - White: Sauvignon Blanc, Gewurztraminer, Riesling, Pinot Gris
      - Sparkling wines.
  - **Central Otago**
    - Central Otago is listed due to it being the most southern wine region in the world and producing some of the best Pinot Noir not only for New Zealand but in direct competition to California's and Oregon's best areas.
    - Central Otago is said to have one of the most scenic wine region around and is certain tourist destination point.
    - Here the climate changes quite a bit, going from the more Maritime to continental and is the only region in New Zealand to offer the type of climate.
    - This is home to New Zealand's Pinot Noir
    - Soil: Alluvial loams
    - Grapes:
      - Red: Pinot Noir
      - White: Sauvignon Blanc, Chardonnay

GRAPES OF UNITED STATES:
A LIST OF GRAPES PROVIDED FOR THE
FOLLOWING STATES.

UNITED STATES: KEY
STATES DISCUSSED IN

UNITED STATES
    California
    Oregon
    Washington
    New York

QUALITY CONTROLS AND LAWS:
- American Viticulture Areas
- TTB
- BATF

The BATF, TTB AND AVA Laws or Regulations
provide Control levels for the UNITED STATES

North America

- **UNITED STATES WINE LAWS**
- **AVA: American Viticulture Area as of 1978** US wineries use this as a geographic pedigree of its wine, to indicate the Appellation of Origin. This must meet federal and state legal requirements. The AVA boundaries are set by geographical features of the surrounding area. The boundaries are defined by the (TTB). The TTB defines AVAs at the request of wineries and other petitioners. There were 193 AVAs as of February, 2009.
- This is a good time to note that unlike most of the European appellation of origin, the AVA only specify the geographical area in which 85% of the grapes used must have been grown. The European AO go much further by limiting the type of grapes grown, method of vinification, yields percentage, minimum alcohol percentage.
- **TTB: The Alcohol and Tobacco Tax and Trade Bureau**, this was abbreviated to TTB and falls under the United States Department of the Treasury. This was a result of the Homeland Security Act of January 24, 2003 where the TTB was established from the ATF. The TTB now oversees in our case much of the wine interest.
- **BATF:** Bureau Alcohol Tobacco Firearms
- AS of 2008 there were 6,368 bonded wineries in the United States.
- First AVA was 1980, surprisingly in Augusta Missouri.
- Labeled with an AVA, 85% of the grapes must come from that AVA
- Labeled by county, 75% of the grapes must come from that county
- Labeled by state, 75% of the grapes must come from that state
- In California, it must be 100%
- Other states may vary in percentage requirement
  - Example Texas is 85%
  - Example Washington is 100%, with exceptions
- In most states, the wine must contain at least 75% of the varietal
- Exception example: Oregon for instance is must be 90%, except when made primarily from cabernet Sauvignon, it's still 75%
- Labeled with a vintage, the wine must have 95% of that year.
- All wines must state the dangers and sulfites contents.

An **appellation (European Term)** is a legally defined and protected geographical indication used to identify where the grapes for a wine were grown. Restrictions other than geographical boundaries, such as what grapes may be grown, maximum grape yields, alcohol level, and other quality factors, may also apply before an appellation name may legally appear on a wine bottle label. The rules that govern appellations are dependent on the country in which the wine was produced.

GRAPES OF CALIFORNIA:

RED	WHITE
CABERNET SAUVIGNON	CHARDONNAY
MERLOT	RIESLING
PINOT NOIR	SAUVIGNON BLANC
SYRAH	CHENIN BLANC
PETITE SIRAH	
ZINFANDEL	

CALIFORNIA: KEY APPELLATIONS DISCUSSED IN REGION:

CALIFORNIA
- Mendocino
- Lake County
- Sonoma
- Napa
- Monterey County
- Central Coast
  - Santa Cruz
  - Santa Clara
  - Mount Harlan
  - Carmel Valley
  - Chalone
- Sierra Foothills
  - Amador County
  - El Dorado County
- Southern region
  - Paso Robles
  - York Mountain
  - Edna Valley
  - Arroyo Grande
  - Santa Maria
  - Santa Ynez
- Los Angeles
  - New AVA's
- Temecula

SOIL: Various

Climate: Moderate Mediterranean

Continental Sierra Foothills

QUALITY CONTROLS AND LAWS:
- American Viticulture Areas
- TTB
- BATF

The Laws provide different levels for
CALIFORNIA

California

Is the leading state for all of the United States and is responsible for approximately 93% of all wine produced is the USA. Gallo is the largest wine producer in the <u>World</u>. By comparison to European wine history, California is definitely the new kid on the block, having said that, we are not without a very colorful history of the wine arena. Early planting goes back to the mid 1700's and are largely due to Franciscan Monks. The establishment of "Missions" brought about much of the planting and development of wine interest. This led to European immigrants bringing cuttings and vineyard progression.

➢ Prohibition: 1920 – 1933 became a very interesting turning point for the United States and from a wine making point, California especially. Outlawing alcohol production and sales was a devastating blow. There were many adamantly oppose to the consumption of alcohol and when the opportunity presented itself, women now voting to abolish the sinful beverage along with many other activist (the Temperance movement very much active in New York and even down under in Australia where they faced equal opposition to alcohol production and use), managed to enact January 1920 Volstead Act (prohibition) until December 1933. 140 wineries out of 800 remained in play by the time the 14 year period ended.

➢ UC Davis: became a major focal point for further study and development of in Enology and Viticulture just after prohibition and soon became one of the leading authorities in the field, assuming much of the interest from University California Berkeley.

➢ California Stats:
  ▪ About ½ million acres of wine producing vineyards now exist in the State of California.
  ▪ As of 2008 there were 2,843 bonded wineries (Gallo being the largest in the world)
  ▪ About 100 grape varieties are grown in the state
  ▪ Early grape from Mexico was known as "Mission" grape and planted in California
  ▪ Early founding wineries:
    • Buena Vista, Charles Krug, Ingelnook, and Schramsberg.
  ▪ Bottle making founded in 1862
  ▪ By the 1960s the winery count was nearly back to where it was prior to Prohibition, nearly 27 years ago.
  ▪ The Paris tasting of 1976 left the French reeling over the Stag's Leap Wine cellars Cabernet Sauvignon and Chateau Montelena's Chardonnay … took first place for the red and white. Château NOW Chateau in the new world

➢ **Grape Varietals:**
➢ **Most planted**
  ▪ **red grape: Cabernet Sauvignon**
  ▪ **white grape: Chardonnay**
    • Before we explore the numerous varieties that do so well within California, let's get the infamous "White Zinfandel" addressed and then move on. The Zinfandel grape is considered to be the "California" grape the other is Petite Sirah, not due to any indigenous attributes but by adoption more than any other way. Zinfandel does

extremely well in California but has been traced back to the recognized Primitivo grape in Italy and then a step further back to origins of Croatia. Having said that, we managed to heighten its awareness quickly in the 70's. Sutter Home in Napa, California, produced the first White Zinfandel wine in 1975 (please refer back to the wine making section in the second chapter for Rose' wines), Sutter Home's White Zinfandel experienced a "stuck fermentation "(this occurs when the yeast goes dormant before the fermentation has completed). This can happen when the yeast dies out before consuming all of the sugar in the <u>Must</u> or possibly when excessive temperatures kill off the yeast or when a <u>Must</u> becomes deficient in the nitrogen, (a food source needed for the yeast to the thrive). The wine maker at the time tasted this somewhat sweet, pink in color wine and felt this was a potential and marketable product. Needless to say, this was not intentional but somewhat of a marketable luck after that fact. They still remain one of the largest producers of White Zinfandel, even though many other wineries have joined the bandwagon.

- **<u>List of many of the Grapes grown in California</u>**

WHITE	**RED**
Chardonnay	Barbera
Chenin Blanc	Cabernet Sauvignon
Gewürztraminer	Carignane
Marsanne	Grenanche
Muscat (Black, orange, white)	Malbec
Pinot Blanc	Merlot
Pinot Gris	Mourvèdre
Riesling	Petite Sirah*
Roussanne	Petit Verdot
Sauvignon Blanc	Pinot Noir
Sémillon	Sangiovese
Viognier	Syrah
	Zinfandel*

*The two adopted California Grape Varietals
California is closer to the use of 100 different varietals

- Taking a close look at California we will tour from the most northern wine growing region to the most southern wine growing region stopping at each region for a short commentary and then moving on.

➢ **MENDOCINO AVA**
- Mendocino is a major Logging industry first, followed by being:
  - The largest percentage of organic vineyards of any county in California.
- **AVA's**
  - **Potter Valley AVA**
    - No wineries in Potter Valley, known for grape production and that will fall into Sauvignon Blanc and the key varietal.
  - **Anderson Valley AVA**
    - **Anderson Valley is divided into two sections**
      - Anderson Valley Bas and Haut (lower and upper)
    - Chardonnay and Pinot Noir are the leading grapes
    - Other grapes would be Gewurztraminer and Riesling.
    - A good amount of Sparkling wine is produced here with the leading areas being:
      - Roederer Estate. (Related to Louis Roederer of the Champagne region of France)
  - **Redwood Valley AVA**
    - The claim to any fame was brought about the Fetzer Vineyard activity and their large planting
    - A key grape is (Zinfandel)
      - Wineries are Lolonis , Fife, Weibel, Frey and a few others.
  - **McDowell Valley AVA**
    - One winery… McDowell Valley Vineyards stands alone here. Typically warm inland area
      - Rhone styles
  - **Cole Ranch AVA**
    - Much of the activity here belongs to Fetzer winery with key grape being Cabernet Sauvignon.
  - **Lake County AVA**
    - There are approximately 34 wineries in Lake County. The first Lake County vineyards were planted in the 1870's. Lake County's climate and altitude permits a reasonable wine grape production just over 1300 feet elevation with an overall cool climate and cooler winter and late growing season.
    - Grapes:
      - Cabernet Sauvignon and Sauvignon Blanc.
      - Bordeaux varietals; Petite Sirah.
      - A Provider of Grapes mostly to:
        - Beringer, Sutter Home and Kendall Jackson
    - Wineries of Note:
      - Guenoc - Langtry, Brassifeld and Steele.
        - Guenoc (Celtic for 'good rock')

- Lady Langtry (Lillie Langtry), an English Actress 1850 that came over from England and started the winery. Petite Sirah and Bordeaux varietals are grown along with a former variety of Bordeaux (Carmenère), which still is grown in France.

> **SONOMA**
- Sonoma is about twice the physical size of Napa. It is Sonoma County where the northern wine region started and then progress over to Napa. Having frequent both Sonoma and Napa, some of the more interesting characteristics are found in the overall life style between the two areas. Sonoma would be the more relaxed, easy going and less glitz and glamour if you will, whereas Napa is a bit faster pace, Limo escorted dining and was the first to seek a hundred dollar bottle of wine and later to seek the two hundred dollar bottle of wine. Having said,
  - Some of the more well known and established wineries of the 1800's and early 1900's are:
  - Buena Vista 1857, Gundlach Bundschu, Sebastiani Family 1904, Kunde Winery, Simi winery 1876; Korbel 1862
- **13 AVA's**
  - Alexander Valley (Cabernet Sauvignon)
  - Bennett Valley
  - Chalk Hill
  - Dry Creek Valley
  - Green Valley
  - Knights Valley
  - Los Carneros
  - Northern Sonoma
  - Rockpile
  - Russian River Valley (Pinot noir and Chardonnay)
  - Sonoma coast
  - Sonoma Valley
  - Sonoma Mountain

> **NAPA VALLEY**
>   ▪ About 55 miles north-east of San Francisco and just east of Sonoma Valley and half the physical size of Sonoma. This area is responsible for approximately 4% of the wines in the state. As mentioned in the section of Sonoma, Napa is known for a number of benchmarks:
>   • 1ˢᵗ $100 bottle of wine and 1ˢᵗ $200 bottle of wine
>   ▪ Robert Mondavi:
>   • I would like acknowledge the efforts of Robert Mondavi of whom I have had the pleasure to converse with on an occasion or two.
>   ▪ Wappo Indians are responsible for the name (Napa) which means "Plenty".
>   ▪ 1ˢᵗ AVA in 1983 in California, and now there are 15 AVA's
>   • Atlas Peak AVA
>   • Calistoga AVA Newest AVA approved by TTB as of November 2009
>   • Chiles Valley AVA
>   • Diamond Mountain District AVA
>   • Howell Mountain AVA
>   • Los Carneros AVA
>   • Mt. Veeder AVA
>   • Oak Knoll District of Napa Valley AVA
>   • Oakville AVA
>   • Rutherford AVA
>   • Spring Mountain District AVA
>   • St. Helena AVA
>   • Stags Leap District AVA
>   • Wild Horse Valley AVA
>   • Yountville AVA

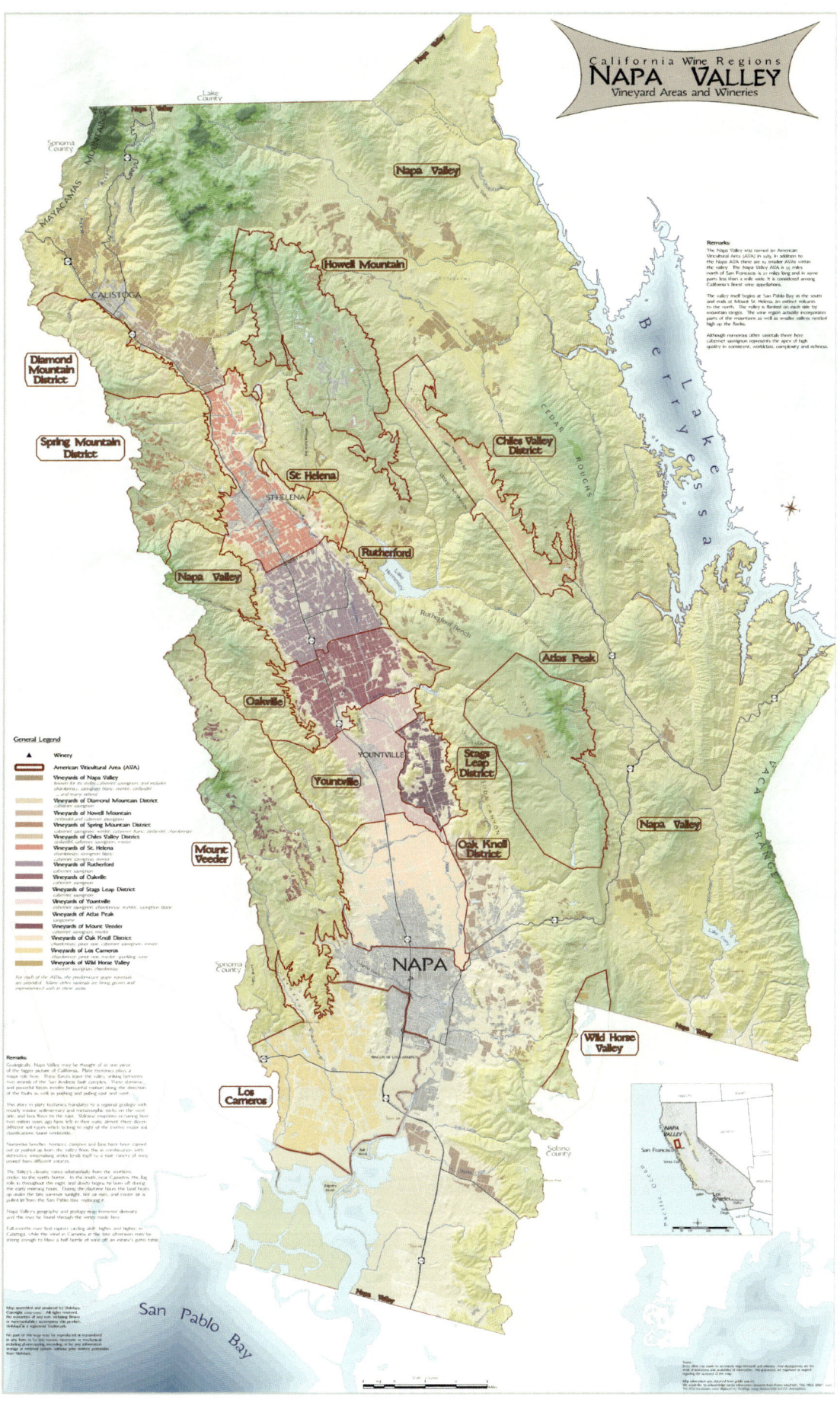

- ➢ **SOUTH OF THE BAY**
  - ▪ **NORTHERN CENTRAL COAST**
    - Monterey County
      - ◆ The largest AVA of the Northern part of California. Matt Kramer makes an interesting note as to the two main division of Monterey. You have the larger more unknown and common effort of Monterey County wine producing regions versus the more micro efforts of individual AVA's that are far more specific in effort and perhaps quality than the large of Monterey. The AVA's of Monterey of the smaller version are listed for your reference.
    - **AVA's of Monterey County**
      - ◆ Arroyo Seca AVA
      - ◆ Chalone AVA
      - ◆ Santa Lucia Highlands AVA
      - ◆ Mount Harlan AVA
      - ◆ Carmel Valley AVA
    - **Santa Cruz Mountains**
  - ▪ There are approximately 70 wineries in Santa Cruz. Much of which started back in the 70's.
  - ▪ The Santa Cruz Mountains Vintners was started in 1973, this was formed to basically map the boundaries for a proposed mountain appellation.
  - ▪ The AVA was approved in 1981 for the appellation of the Santa Cruz Mountain range.
    - **A few Santa Cruz vineyards noted:**
      - ◆ Bonny Doon vineyard is very well known of this area.
      - ◆ David Bruce
      - ◆ Mount Eden vineyard
      - ◆ Ridge (yes you will find Ridge in a number of California locations)
    - **Santa Clara Valley AVA**
      - ◆ **Santa Clara AVA includes**
        - o Pacheco Pass AVA
        - o San Ysidro AVA
      - ◆ Even fewer vineyard are located in Santa Clara Valley most obtain fruit from other regions. There are 25 wineries in the area.
      - ◆ Grapes most noted:
        - o Chardonnay
        - o Cabernet Sauvignon
        - o Merlot
        - o Zinfandel.
    - **A few Santa Clara vineyards noted:**
      - ◆ Clos LaChance Wines
      - ◆ Fortino Winery
      - ◆ Hecker Pass Winery
      - ◆ Solis Winery

CENTRAL COAST
California
Wine Regions

MONTEREY

Paso Robles

PASO ROBLES

Atascadero

YORK MTN

SAN   LUIS

US101

Morro Bay

OBISPO

Baywood-Los Osos

San Luis
Obispo

EDNA VALLEY

ARROYO GRANDE VALLEY

Grover Beach   Arroyo Grande

Nipomo

SANTA MARIA VALLEY

Santa Maria

Orcutt

US101

SANTA YNEZ VALLEY

SANTA

Lompoc

SANTA YNEZ VALLEY

BARBARA

Pacific Ocean

San Francisco

Los Angeles

No part of this map may be
reproduced or transmitted in any
form or by any means, electronic or
mechanical, including photocopying,
recording, or by any information
storage or retrieval system, without
prior written permission from VinMaps.
VinMaps is a registered trademark.

N
W   E
S

0   15   30 Kilometers

18.64 Miles

Goleta   Santa Barbara

- ➢ **CENTRAL / SOUTH CENTRAL**
  - ▪ **Paso Robles**
    - This is an area that as been noted for other wine country. Paso Robles have stood in the shadows of regions like Napa and Sonoma far too long. Paso Robles sits almost exactly half way between Los Angeles and the Napa / Sonoma wine country. As far as an AVA is concern. This area is all reality one AVA, at this point no one has really established boundaries for this area. Paso Robles in its full name is (El Paso de Robles) "the pass of Oaks".
    - Grapes most noted:
      - ◆ Zinfandel (has really taken off and become a start for many of the wineries)
      - ◆ Cabernet Sauvignon
      - ◆ Syrah
      - ◆ Merlot
      - ◆ Pinot Noir
      - ◆ Rhone varietals are doing quite well both white and red.
      - ◆ Chardonnay
  - ▪ **A few Paso Robles vineyards noted:**
    - Dark Star Cellars
    - Eberly Winery
    - EOS Estate Winery
    - Justin Vineyards and Winery
    - Meridian Vineyards
    - Robert Hall Winery
    - Tobin James Cellars
    - Turley Wine Cellars
    - Wineward Vineyards
    - York Mountain Winery
  - ▪ **Edna Valley**

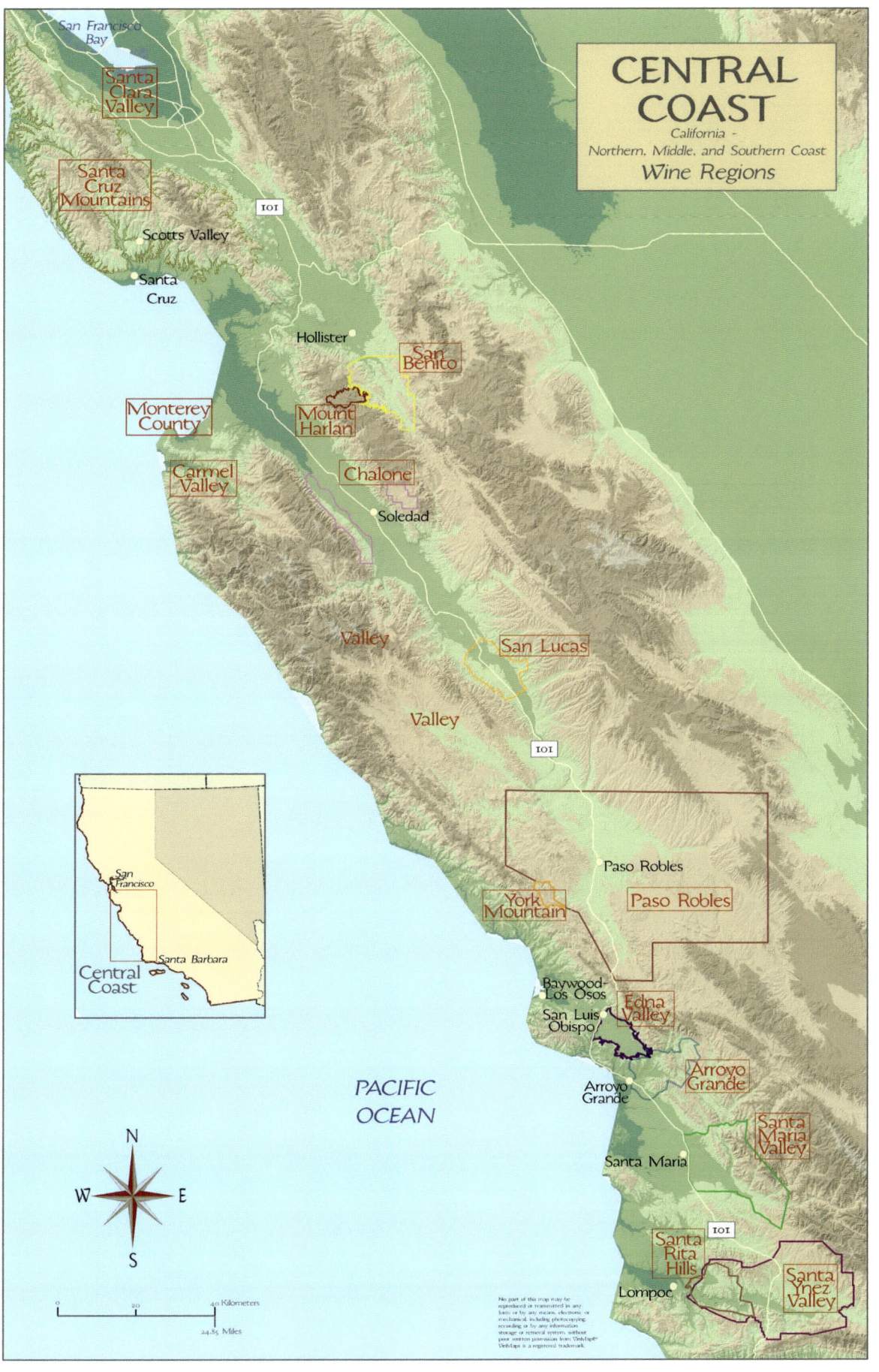

CENTRAL COAST

California -
Northern, Middle, and Southern Coast

Wine Regions

San Francisco Bay

Santa Clara Valley

Santa Cruz Mountains

Scotts Valley

Santa Cruz

Hollister

San Benito

Monterey County

Mount Harlan

Carmel Valley

Chalone

Soledad

Valley

San Lucas

Valley

San Francisco

Santa Barbara

Central Coast

Paso Robles

Paso Robles

York Mountain

Baywood-Los Osos

San Luis Obispo

Edna Valley

Arroyo Grande

Arroyo Grande

Santa Maria Valley

Santa Maria

PACIFIC OCEAN

Santa Rita Hills

Santa Ynez Valley

Lompoc

N
W E
S

0   20   40 Kilometers
24.85 Miles

- **Just south of Paso Robles lies Edna Valley AVA. This is another wine region that doesn't get the attention it deserves. It is a bit smaller and cooler than Paso Robles.**
- **There are a various soils in the region but mostly calcareous** from long time pass sea beds, clay and loam.
- Grapes most noted:
  - Chardonnay
  - Pinot Noir
- **Arroyo Grande**
  - Arroyo Grande is just south of Edna Valley and have very little difference in climate or soil conditions

- ➢ **Santa Barbara County**
  - **Santa Maria Valley AVA**
    - Basically maritime climate conditions and not really noted for any real outstanding wines other than Chardonnay. Here you will find the "California" style of chardonnay, rich and opulent and in many cases a crowd pleaser for those seeking the luscious ripe fruit and oak mouth fill.
    - Grape
      - Chardonnay
  - **A few Paso Robles vineyards noted:**
    - Cambria
    - Dierberg Santa Maria Vineyard
    - Loma Verde Vineyard
    - Flood Vineyard
  - **Santa Ynez Valley AVA**
    - Rolling hills and a wide range of temperatures and a picturesque view in every direction is what you get in this AVA valley. This is another area within California that has not received the attention due but is now growing with admiration and expectancy. Santa Ynez and Los Olivos (the olives) great wines.
    - Grapes most noted:
      - Chardonnay
      - Pinot Noir
      - Cabernet Sauvignon
      - Merlot
      - Sauvignon Blanc
      - Syrah and (Rhone varietals)
  - **Santa Rita Hills AVA (most recent) as of 2001**
    - This is the new kid on the block. Santa Rita Hills has come into its own fame through the grapes of Chardonnay and especially Pinot Noir.
  - **A few Paso Robles vineyards noted:**
    - Sea Smoke (obtaining great attention)
    - Sanford & Benedict Vineyard
    - Cargasacchi Vineyards

- ➢ SIERRA FOOTHILLS AVA
  - ▪ Some of the interesting and unique history of the Sierra Foothills is based on the 1849 Gold Rush. This is the era sparked much of the planting to accommodate the local seeking drink after a full day of gold seeking. Much more inland, the climate
  - ▪ Amador County
    - • First on the scene in 1970
    - • Zinfandel
    - ➢ El Dorado County
- ➢ SOUTH COAST
  - ▪ Los Angeles
    - • New AVA's are now included in the region of Los Angeles
    - • Certainly not on the running level with wineries situated from Santa Barbara and moving north but new wineries and growers and making a mark for the Los Angeles County. There are now 5 registered wineries with AVA's or Proposed AVA's, in addition, there are over 33 wine growers nearing several 100 acres of vines planted.
      - ◆ Agua Dolce
      - ◆ Antelope Valley winery
      - ◆ Leona Valley winery
  - ▪ Temecula
    - • It would be remised not to mention the wineries in Temecula. Reviewing a number of textbooks I've use in Class, most for various reasons have not included the area of Temecula in the context. Well Temecula is the down south wine area and have not quite gain the attention of those residing farther north. Temecula was plagued with the unfortunate residence the Glassy-winged sharpshooter a serious new pest in California. It is a particular threat to California vineyards due to its ability to spread *Xylella fastidiosa* the bacterium that causes Pierce's disease. Pierce's disease kills grapevines, and there are no effective treatments for it.

Wineries for reference and Note:

Baily Vineyard & Winery

Briar Rose Winery

Callaway Vineyard & Winery

Churon Winery

Cougar Vineyard & Winery

Doffo Vineyard & Winery

Falkner Winery

Filsinger Winery

Foote Print Winery

Hart Winery

Keyways Vineyard & Winery

Leonesse Cellars

Maurice Car'rie Vineyard

Miramonte Winery Mount Palomar Winery

Oak Mountain Winery

Palumbo Family Vineyards & Winery

The Ponte Family Estate Winery

Robert Renzoni Vineyards

South Coast Winery Resort & Spa

Stuart Cellars

Temecula Vineyard Estates

Thorton Winery

Villa di Calabro Winery & Olive Oil Co.

Wiens Family Cellars

Wilson Creek Winery

California

Potter Valley

Clear Lake

Anderson Valley

Knights Valley

McDowell Valley

Guenoc Valley

Alexander Valley

Napa Valley

Dry Creek

Clarksburg

Russian River

El Dorado

Sonoma

Amador Count

Los Carneros

Lodi

Green Valley

Livermore Valley

Santa Cruz Mountains

Santa Clara Valley

Mount Harlan

Chalone

Carmel Valley

Arroyo Seco

Monterey County

Paso Robles

Santa Maria Valley

Santa Ynez Valley

Los Angeles

Temecula

Arroyo Grande

York Mountain

Edna Valley

Arroyo Grande

GRAPES OF WASHINGTON STATE:

RED	WHITE
MERLOT	SAUVIGNON BLANC
CABERNET SAUVIGNON	CHARDONNAY
RIESLING	

WASHINGTON STATE: KEY APPELLATIONS DISCUSSED IN REGION:

WASHINGTON STATE
1)   Columbia Valley
    i)   Walla Walla
   ii)   Yakima Valley
2)   Puget Sound
3)   Red Mountain

SOIL: Sandy loam, Volcanic

CLIMATE: Maritime mostly much of the wine area is dry and warm.

QUALITY CONTROLS AND LAWS:
- American Viticultural Areas
- TTB
- BATF
- Washington Wine Quality Alliance (WWQA)

The Laws provide different levels for WASHINGTON STATE

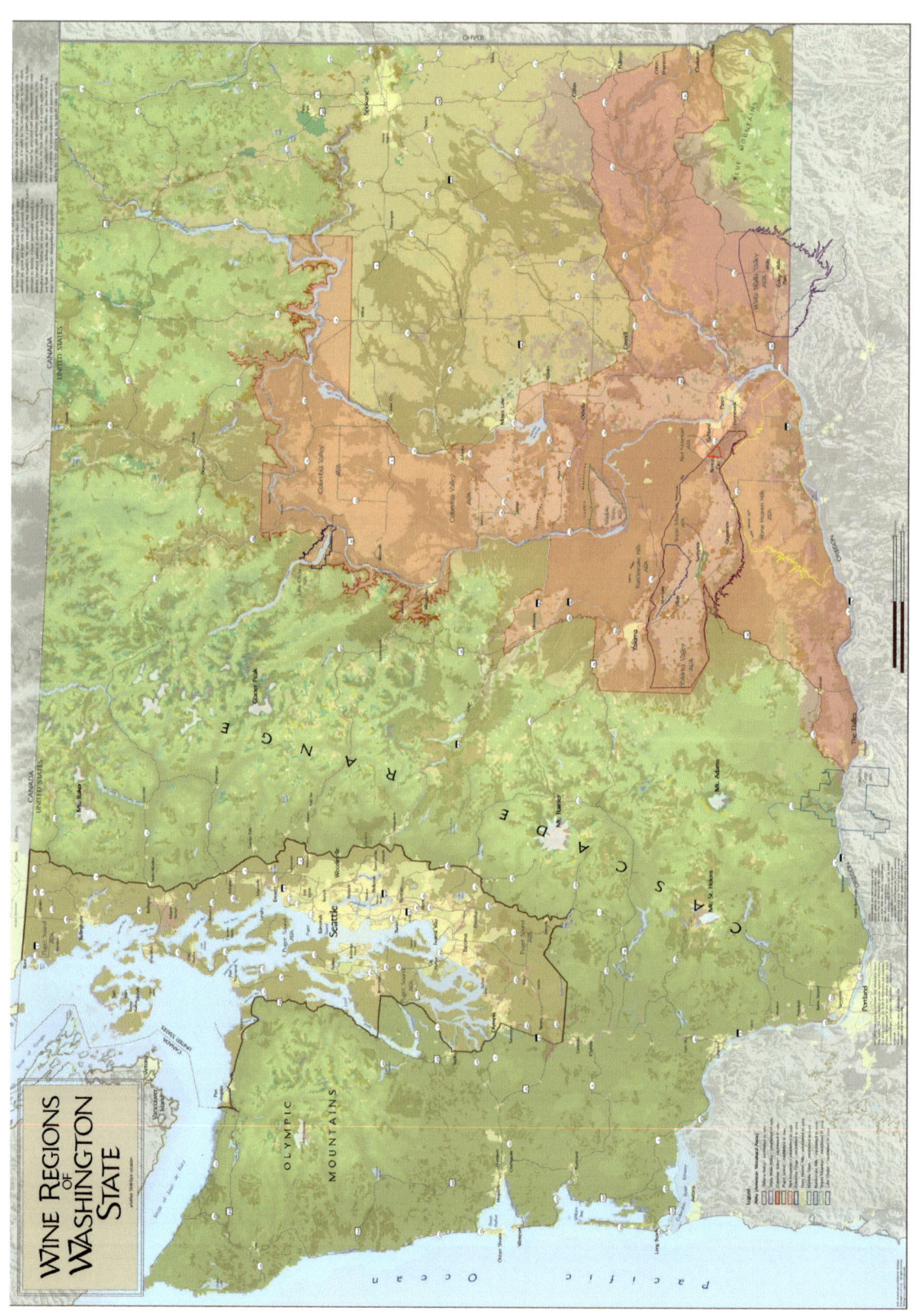

WINE REGIONS OF WASHINGTON STATE

Washington State

Washington is the second largest producer of wine in the United States, which means, obviously to California.

- **WWQA**: In 1999 a trade organization was formed to promote the wine industry and set quality standards for the members of the organization. The **WWQA** is not a state mandate but a voluntary membership to assist the members is providing a practice level to assure quality recognized standards. The members must comply to the following regulations:
    - Reserve wines are not to exceed 10% of winery's production or 3,000 cases. (Note: this is not unique to Washington many other countries following this 10% rule).
    - 100% of the grapes must come from Washington or the percentage of the source should be listed on the label.
    - And as mentioned in Chapter 1, to comply with the appellation recognition and not use terms such as Champagne, Chablis, Burgundy..etc.

Grapes of the area:

White	Red
Riesling	Merlot
Chardonnay	Cabernet Sauvignon
Sauvignon Blanc	Syrah
Gewürztraminer	Cabernet Franc
Chenin Blanc	
Muscat Canelli	

❖ Columbia Valley

➢ This is the largest of the appellations encompassing:
- Yakima Valley
  - Yakima Valley is an appellation in its own right but lies under the umbrella of Columbia Valley. It is cooler than Columbia Valley with some extreme cold winters.
- Walla Walla
  - The smallest district straddling the Washington / Oregon border. The dominant grape varieties are:
    - Merlot
    - Chardonnay
    - Cabernet Sauvignon
    - Sangiovese
    - Syrah

❖ Puget Sound

➢ Is the newest of Washington's Appellation's (officially recognized in 1995). This AVA extends from Canada southward. The wineries are few and far between. Not favored with ideal growing conditions most of the fruit is sourced from Columbia, Yakima and Walla Walla.

GRAPES OF OREGON:

RED	WHITE
PINOT NOIR	PINOT GRIS
MERLOT	GEWÜRZTRAMINER
CABERNET SAUVIGNON	CHARDONNAY
	RIESLING
	PINOT BLANC

OREGON: KEY APPELLATIONS DISCUSSED IN REGION:

OREGON
1) Willamette Valley
   i) Dundee Hills:
   ii) Argyle:
   iii) Domain Drouhin
2) Umpqua Valley

3) Rogue Valley
   i) Illnois Valley
   ii) Applegate Valley
   iii) The Rouge River

SOIL: Chalk, Clay, Silt and Limestone

CLIMATE: About 40 inches of rain per year. Cool. Moderate temperatures

QUALITY CONTROLS AND LAWS:
- American Viticultural Areas
- TTB
- BATF
- Oregon Liquor Control Commission (OLCC)

The Laws provide different levels for OREGON

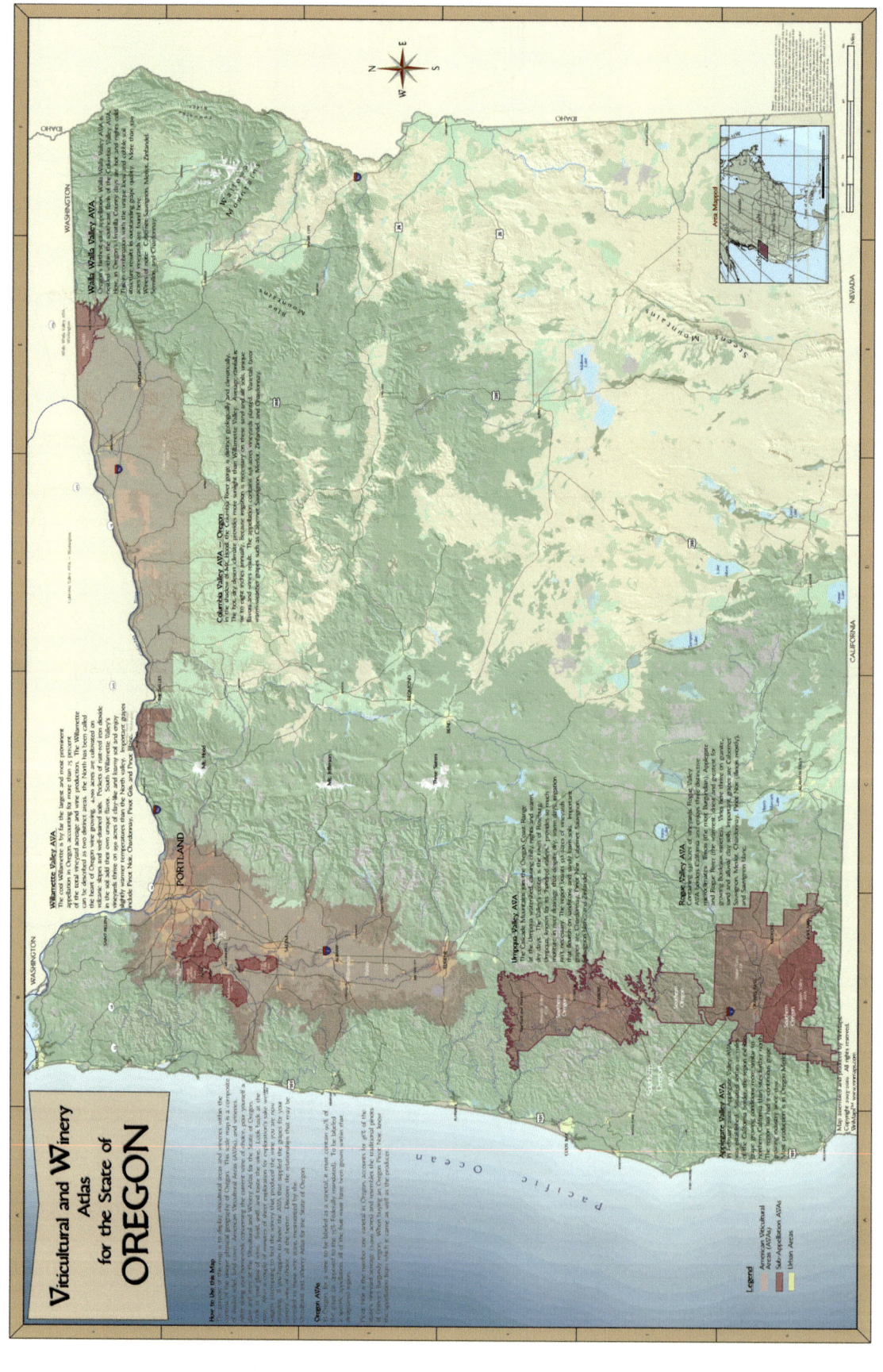

Viticultural and Winery Atlas for the State of OREGON

❖ Oregon

- Oregon came much into play in 1980, following much praise of its Pinot Noir. By 1994 Oregon was synonymous with Pinot Noir. Not to say that this began their wine growing establishment. Oregon has been around for decades, although they hold 1961 as their date of birth.
- **Oregon's wine Laws:**
  - The Oregon Liquor Control Commission (OLCC) was enacted in 1977 that set rules as follows:
    - Estate wines must be within 5 miles of the winery.
    - State law requires 90% minimum content of whatever grape variety is named on the label (except Cabernet Sauvignon which must be 75%).
    - And as mentioned in Chapter 1, to comply with the appellation recognition and not use terms such as Champagne, Chablis, Burgundy..etc.

GRAPES Varietals

RED	**WHITE**
PINOT NOIR	PINOT GRIS
MERLOT	GEWÜRZTRAMINER
CABERNET SAUVIGNON	RIESLING
	CHARDONNAY

➢ **Willamette Valley:**
- The largest and most important wine growing region, stretching from Portland north to Eugene south. There are 3 key Sub-regions
  - Dundee Hills:
  - Argyle:
  - Domain Drouhin:

➢ **Umpqua Valley:**
- This AVA is a small historical agriculture area centered on Roseburg in the valley along the Umpqua River. In 1961 Richard Sommer established Hill Crest Vineyard the oldest continuing operating vineyard in Oregon. Warmer and dryer than Willamette Valley in the north, Umpqua Valley is suited to a wide range of varietals because of its cooler sites inland.
  - Note: Henry Estate Winery: (known for the development of the Scott Henry Trellising system design).

➢ Rogue Valley
- The southern most wine region in Oregon. It stretches from the California border to Grants Pass. There are 3 distinctively different Sub-Regions (the term appellations are

often used but not completely relevant or applicable when speaking in terms of new world), provide a wide range of climate.

➢ **The Illinois Valley:**
- To the west and has a cooler climate with Pacific Ocean influence. Key grapes are Pinot Noir and Pinot Gris)

➢ **The Applegate Valley:**
- In the center has a much warmer climate. Key grapes are (Merlot and Cabernet Sauvignon)

➢ **The Rouge River**
- As the eastern border and offers a Bordeaux varietal

GRAPES OF NEW YORK:

RED	WHITE
PINOT NOIR	SEYVAL BLANC
CATAWBA	VIDAL BLANC
NIAGARA	ISABELLA
MERLOT	DELEWARE
CABERNET FRANC	VIGNOLES
	CHARDONNAY
	RIESLING

NEW YORK: KEY APPELLATIONS DISCUSSED IN REGION:

NEW YORK
a) Finger Lakes
b) Hudson River Valley
c) Lake Erie
d) Long Island

SOIL: Gravel; Clay; Shale

Climate: Atlantic influence; humid; Mediterranean and Maritime.

QUALITY CONTROLS AND LAWS:
- American Viticultural Areas
- TTB
- BATF

The Laws provide different levels for NEW YORK

New York
Wine Regions

CANADA
● Toronto

ONTARIO
Niagara
On-The-Lake
● St. Catharines
Niagara
On-The-Lake

Niagara
Escarpment

● Buffalo

Lake Erie

Lake Erie

Lake Ontario

● Rochester

Finger
Lakes

Cayuga Lk.
Seneca Lk.
Canandaigua Lk.
Keuka Lk.

N E W

Y O R K

P E N N S Y L V A N I A

Lake Erie - Wine Region

● Harrisburg

● Philadelphia

● Trenton

● Newark

● Albany

Hudson
River

● Hartford

North Fork

The Hamptons

Long Island

● New York
● Brooklyn
New York

N
W   E
S

0   45   90 Kilometers
0   55.9 Miles

CANADA

Chicago ● Detroit
● Boston

● New York
Baltimore ●

Area Mapped

❖ New York

- As one of North America's top 4 wine producing regions we will include this as part of this textbook. New York comes as a big surprise to most students ready to engage in wine studies. Please keep in mind that New York along with a few other states on the east coast accommodated settlers that as early the 1600's brought cuttings over for planting, most quite unsuccessful. New York's wine country covers the entire distance of New York. A couple of centuries later both the Vitis Vinifera and American grapes offered promise and continue as of today. The Vitis Vinifera accounts for approximately 10% of New York's wine production. New York is much more known for their Hybrids, these are other Vitis species, two or more hybridized to yield the best of both worlds.

➤ **There are four major wine growing regions in New York.**

➤ The Finger Lakes AVA: in the west-central
  - The Finger Lakes wine region is located in the heart of the larger geographical area.

➤ The Hudson Valley AVA: in eastern region
  - North of New York City is the Hudson River wine region, which is one of America's most historic wine regions. Moderated temperatures by the Hudson River, presents a more maritime climate. The Hudson River wine region has proved favorable to Chardonnay and Cabernet Franc.

➤ The Lake Erie AVA: on the western end
  - The largest grape growing county outside of California is the Lake Erie Viticultural Area, also known as Chautauqua, with 20,000 acres

➤ Long Island Region AVA:
  - The Long Island wine region is the newest and fastest growing wine region, located about 100 miles east of New York City. The Long Island Region is surrounded by the Atlantic Ocean on the south and Long Island Sound on the north. The Island offers a long growing season where merlots, chardonnays, and other European classics do well.

```
GRAPES: European
White                    Red
Riesling                 Pinot Noir
Chardonnay               Cabernet Sauvignon
Gewürztraminer           Merlot
                         Cabernet France
                         Pinot Noir
```

```
Hybrid Varietals
White                    Red
Seyval Blanc             Catawba
Vidal Blanc
Niagara
Delaware
Vignoles
```

❖ **GRAPES: American Hybrids:**

➢ **Seyval Blanc:** (French-American) A French-American hybrid grape that can be used to make high quality white wines of various styles. Crisp, fruity dry versions have sometimes been likened to French "Chablis" in aroma and taste. Grown extensively in the colder northern temperate zones of N. America and Europe.

➢ **Vidal Blanc:** Popular French-American hybrid white wine grape with fruity, floral flavors and good balance descended from the Ugni Blanc of France, (aka Trebbiano of Italy). Made in a variety of styles - (i.e: Dry to sweet including late-harvest dessert style and ice wines). Cool region grapes vinified in a Rhine/Mosel manner are said to have a Riesling-like character.

➢ **Catawba:** A Native American - ("vitis labrusca") - grape used to produce sweet white, red and rose' wines distinguished by a so-called "foxy" component. Commonly grown in the Eastern U.S. and Canada. New York state wineries produce large amounts of sparkling wine from this grape. It is also quite popular when made into an ultra-sweet "ice-wine".

➢ **Isabella:** French-American hybrid grape grown on limited acreages in New York State. Also still found in colder regions of Eastern Europe. Derived from a native vitis labrusca grape of N. America and an unknown vinifera and probably created by random pollination as a result of the 18th century attempts to establish European vines in the U.S. Rapidly being removed and replaced by varieties that lack the obtrusive "foxy" taste and flavor of this grape.

➢ **Delaware:** A Native American hybrid grape variety used to make dry, sweet and sparkling white wines of good quality and mild "foxy" character. Commonly grown in the Eastern U.S. where it has considerable popularity when made into "ice-wine".

➢ **Niagara:** Native American hybrid grape used to create popular white wines with strong "grapey" flavor, usually sweet finished, but also found in dry versions. Possibly one of the few hybrids that will remain popular in the U.S. because of a wide consumer base created after World War II. Vine plantings are mainly in the Eastern and Mid-West regions of the U.S.

➢ **Vignoles:** (aka Ravat 51) is a complex hybrid wine grape variety produced from a cross made by J.F. Ravat of two grapes, Seibel 8665 and Pinot de corton). This is only mentioned due to the use of this grape as a major contributor to Ice Wine.

Test your Knowledge

The following questions for any given chapter utilize three methods of questioning; True or False; Multiple Choice; or fill in the Blank(s). All three methods are standard practice for typical quizzes, tests and exams. My thoughts regarding this are: You have a 50% chance with "True or False" method; a 20 -25% chance with multiple choice and pretty much you know it or not with the fill-in-the-blank(s). The use of "Fill-in-the-blank" questions, can present the possibilities for some confusion, misinterpretation, or ambiguity. Having said that, I feel the fill in the blank exercise does offer a very clear suggestion of a working knowledge of the material.

❖ Enology and Viticulture (Chapter 2)

TERMINOLOGY MATCHING

1) ___Grape solids (skin and pulp) that separate from juice of crushed grapes (must) and tend to float on the surface

2) ___Device for breaking grapes berry skins to permit juice extraction

3) ___One of two simple fermentable sugars present in grapes

4) ___A solid form or source of sulfur dioxide

5) ___Juice or wine that separates freely from grape solids without the use of mechanical or other energy.

6) ___Process for mixing juice with skins in red wine fermentation to extract greater color.

7) ___Mixture containing grape skins, seeds, pulp, spent yeast cells and small grape particulate matter.

8) ___Removal of excess potassium bitartrate or Tartaric acid to prevent its crystallization and precipitation in wine stored under cold conditions

9) ___Device for or process of separating grape stem from berries

10) ___Phenolic compounds naturally occurring in grapes and wines; responsible for astringency and / or bitter flavors in wine

11) ___Adding sugar to must of juice before fermentation to make up for deficiencies

12) ___The empty space that develops in bottles or casks as wine evaporates

13) ___The addition of various materials that remove certain wine constituents for improved wine quality or stability.

14) ___Conversion of grape sugar by yeast to ethanol and carbon dioxide

15) ___Conversion of Malic acid in wine into Lactic acid and carbon dioxide by certain lactic acid bacteria

16) ___Process whereby grape juice or wine constituents react with oxygen, resulting in undesirable odor and flavor changes.

A   Cold stabilization
B   Bentonite
C   Chaptalization
D   Oxidation
E   Fructose or Glucose
F   Ullage
G   Must
H   Fermentation
I   Fining
J   Pumping Over or Punching down
K   Cap
L   Crusher
M   Free - Run
N   Topping-up
O   Tannins
P   Stemmer or de-stemming
Q   Lees
R   Metabisulfite Potassium

❖ **Enology and Viticulture (Chapter 2)**

1) True or False
   a) _____ A Champagne labeled Extra Dry would be, sweeter than Brut?
   b) _____ Vitis Vinifera varietals can be grafted on to various Root Stock?
   c) _____ Making red wine, you ferment the <u>Must</u> before pressing?
   d) _____ The <u>Canopy</u> is the leaf portion of the vine?
   e) _____ The <u>Trellis</u> is a type of support for the grape vines?

2) Which of the following species of vine does the majority of wine making grapes fall under.
   a) Vitis Labrusca
   b) Vitis Vinifera
   c) Vitis Riparia
   d) Vitis Rupestris
   e) Vitis Rotundifolia

3) Which one of the following is used as a fining agent
   a) Sulfur dioxide
   b) Carbon dioxide
   c) Yeast
   d) Bentonite

4) What is added to the <u>Must</u> to start fermentation
   a) Sulfur dioxide
   b) Carbon dioxide
   c) Yeast
   d) Bentonite

5) Racking is a process by which:
   a) Mixing or pumping the wine over is done.
   b) The wine is removed off the lees or sediment
   c) Additional sugar is added to the wine for better fermentation
   d) Sulfur dioxide is added to stop the fermentation process.

6) Tannin is a substance found in
   a) The flesh or meat of the grape
   b) The seeds only
   c) The skin and stalks and aids in the preservation of the wine
   d) The juice of the wine and helps increase sweetness

7) Better suited soils for a vineyard have the following
   a) Very high concentrations of potassium
   b) Very fertile and rich in calcium
   c) Very good drainage
   d) Very poor drainage

8) Name the 5 styles of wine
   a) _____
   b) _____
   c) _____
   d) _____
   e) _____

9) In respect to making red wine, white wines are typically fermented under the following conditions.
   a) At the same temperature as red wine.
   b) At a much higher temperature than red wine.
   c) At a lower temperature than red wine
   d) During fermentation, the temperature doesn't matter

10) NAME 4 RED GRAPES
   a) _____
   b) _____
   c) _____
   d) _____

11) NAME 4 WHITE GRAPES
   a) _____
   b) _____
   c) _____
   d) _____

12) Vines that are full with large berries and many bunches are better suited for
   a) Very expensive wines and higher quality
   b) Inexpensive, common wines
   c) Wines with intense flavors and complexity.
   d) In general, grapes destined for desert wines.

13) Which of the following best describe Mediterranean climate
   a) Characterize by warm summers and mid winters.
   b) Climate with warm summers and mid winters most of the rainfall occurs in winter.
   c) Extreme temperatures in both winter and summer.
   d) Characterize by cool summers and cold winters.

14) The Purpose of Malolactic fermentation is to
   a) Increase the acidity of the wine
   b) Increase the good flavors of the wine
   c) Decrease the acidity of the in the finished wine
   d) Complete the conversion from sugar to alcohol

15) Malolatic fermentation is the result of the action of
   a) Yeast
   b) Bacteria
   c) Chemicals
   d) Light

16) The word or indication of "Brut" on a bottle of Champagne indicates that it is:
   a) Inexpensive
   b) High in Acid
   c) Low in Tannins
   d) Dry
   e) Very sweet

17) Which of the following is the correct list of grapes used to make Champagne
   a) Sauvignon Blanc, Chardonnay, Pinot Noir
   b) Chardonnay, Muscat, Pinot Noir
   c) Chardonnay, Pinot Meunier, Pinot Noir
   d) Cabernet Sauvignon, Pinot Noir, Chardonnay

18) In terms of Non-Vintage Champagne, which is true for Vintage Champagne
   a) It is made from black grapes ONLY
   b) Is only made in California
   c) The base wines come from a single year
   d) The wine is dryer than Non-Vintage
   e) It is made from white grapes ONLY.

19) Please name three growing conditions that can occur in the vineyards that will allow the process for making sweet wine.
   a) _____
   b) _____
   c) _____

20) Please list the six typically accepted levels of Champagne or Sparkling wine indicating (Dryness or Sweetness).
   a) _____
   b) _____
   c) _____
   d) _____
   e) _____
   f) _____

❖ France (Chapter 3)

1) French wine designations are (from the highest quality level to the basic).
   a) Vin de table, VDQS, Vin de pays, AOC
   b) VDQS, Vin de pays, AOC, Vin de table,
   c) AOC, Vin de table, VDQS, Vin de pays,
   d) AOC, VDQS, Vin de pays, Vin de table

2) Name 6 key Regions in France for wine production
   a) _____
   b) _____
   c) _____
   d) _____
   e) _____
   f) _____

3) The top rated vineyards in Burgundy is a
   a) Grand Cru
   b) Premier Cru
   c) Commune
   d) Clos

4) Please list the five accepted red Bordeaux varietals
   a) _____
   b) _____
   c) _____
   d) _____
   e) _____

5) The grape use to produce Chablis is
   a) Chasselas
   b) Pinot Noir
   c) Sauvignon Blanc
   d) Chardonnay

6) The grape used to produce Beaujolais is
   a) Chardonnay
   b) Pinot Noir
   c) Gamay
   d) Aligote

7) The Côte d'Or is divided into regions
   a) Chalonnaise and Maconnais
   b) Côte de Nuits and Côte de Beaune

    c) Dijon and Lyons

    d) Côte de Nuits and Côte de Charmes

    e) None of the above

8) Please name the four quality levels used in Burgundy

    a) _____

    b) _____

    c) _____

    d) _____

9) The main red grape of the Northern Rhone is

    a) Gamay

    b) Syrah

    c) Grenanche

    d) Cabernet Sauvignon

10) Some say Syrah reaches its peak expression in

    a) Gigondas

    b) Châteauneuf-du-Pape

    c) Condrieu

    d) Hermitage

11) Name 5 Varietals that can be used for Châteaneuf-du-Pape :

    a) _____

    b) _____

    c) _____

    d) _____

    e) _____

12) Which of the varietals listed is the most planted grape in the Bordeaux region

    a) Cabernet Sauvignon

    b) Cabernet Franc

    c) Merlot

    d) Syrah

    e) Grenache

13) Wines of Sancerre would use what grape

    a) _____

14) Which of the following varietals most define the wines from Pomerol
   a) Chardonnay
   b) Merlot
   c) Cabernet Sauvignon
   d) Cabernet Franc
   e) Sauvignon Blanc

15) The key soil type noted for Burgundy is:
   a) _____

16) Which of the following wines is most noted for the use of Carbonic Maceration
   a) Champagne
   b) Sancerre
   c) Beaujolais
   d) Vouvray
   e) Chablis

17) Which of the following varietals is NOT a noble grape of Alsace
   a) Pinot Gris
   b) Chardonnay
   c) Gewürztraminer
   d) Riesling

18) Please name the term use for a late harvest wine produced in Alsace
   a) _____

19) Which of the following varietals is typically used for dry, un-oaked, white wines with vegetal flavors and high acidity?
   a) Merlot
   b) Chardonnay
   c) Sauvignon Blanc
   d) Pinot Noir

❖ Italy (Chapter 4)

1) The top level of quality among Italian wines, by law is
    a) DOC
    b) IGT
    c) AOC
    d) DOCG

2) Barbaresco is made from
    a) Barolo
    b) Sangiovese
    c) Cortese
    d) Nebbiolo

3) The main red grape in Tuscany is
    a) Nebbiolo
    b) Sangiovese
    c) Trebbiano
    d) Canaiolo

4) Chianti is made primarily of what grape.
    a) _____

5) Name 4 key regions in the North-west area of Italy
    a) _____
    b) _____
    c) _____
    d) _____

6) Name the fortified wine that is primarily made in Sicily.
    a) _____

7) Name 3 key regions in the North-east area of Italy
    a) _____
    b) _____
    c) _____

8) Name two styles of wine made in the Valpolicella region that utilized dried grapes that are placed on straw mats to reduce the water content. The wines are make dry and sweet.
    a) _____
    b) _____

9) What is the main grape used in the Valpolicella region for much of the wines.

    a) _____

10) Name two sub-regions of the Veneto area

    a) _____

    b) _____

11) Name two of Tuscany's most important red wines:

    a) _____

    b) _____

12) Name one of the Fantasy named "Super-Tuscans"

    a) _____

13) Name 3 regions in the Southern area of Italy

    a) _____

    b) _____

    c) _____

❖ Spain and Portugal (Chapter 5)

1) Name 5 Regions in Spain for wine production
   a) _____
   b) _____
   c) _____
   d) _____
   e) _____

2) Name the dominant variety in Rias Baixas:
   a) Airen
   b) Tempranillo
   c) Vinho Verde
   d) Albarino

3) The main grape for Sherry production is
   a) Tempranillo
   b) Palomino
   c) Airen
   d) Alvarino

4) Name two styles of Sherry
   a) _____
   b) _____

5) Name two of the key grapes use for Cava in Spain
   a) _____
   b) _____

6) Name two key grape varietals most recognized for the wine of Rioja
   a) _____
   b) _____

7) Name a key region in the North-West area of Spain
   a) _____

8) Which of the following is a true statement?
   a) Most of the wines from Rueda utilized the Tempranillo.
   b) Most of the wines of the southern region of Spain are sparkling
   c) The key soil of the Jerez region is named Albariza
   d) The wines of the North-western part of Spain are primarily red?

9) Vintage Port is
    a) Made every year
    b) Typically only made in special years, when approved by (committee).
    c) Never made
    d) Made whenever the crop is good

10) The majority of wine that comes from Vinho Verde is
    a) White
    b) Red
    c) Green
    d) Rose'

11) Portuguese viticulture uses grapes
    a) Indigenous to Portugal
    b) From Western Europe
    c) From Eastern Europe
    d) None of the above

12) Name two styles of Port
    a) _____
    b) _____

13) Which of the following varietals is most common for Port (Portugal)
    a) Cabernet Sauvignon
    b) Touriga National
    c) Malvasia
    d) Vinho Verde
    e) Torrontés

❖ Germany (Chapter 6)

1) Name the styles of German QmP wines in term of sweetness ; from the driest to the sweetest:
    a) _____
    b) _____
    c) _____
    d) _____
    e) _____

2) Name 5 Regions in Germany for wine production
    a) _____
    b) _____
    c) _____
    d) _____
    e) _____

3) The most noble variety of German wines is
    a) Gewürztraminer
    b) Silvaner
    c) Müller-Thurgau
    d) Riesling

4) The German name for Pinot Noir
    a) Spätburgunder
    b) Blaubuergunder
    c) Grauburgunder
    d) Burgunder

5) Most dominate red wine region in Germany
    a) Mosel
    b) Ahr
    c) Pfalz
    d) Rheingau

6) Most noted and recognized wine region of Germany
    a) Baden
    b) Ahr
    c) Hessiche Bergstrasse
    d) Mosel
    e) Nahe

❖ Austria (Chapter 7)

1) Most popular and important grape varietal in Austria
   a) _____

2) Name two of the major key region of the four for Austria
   a) _____
   b) _____

3) Which of the following is not likely a varietal for Austria
   a) Riesling
   b) Trebbiano
   c) Weissburgunder
   d) Zweigelt

4) Which of the following is not a true statement?
   a) Much of the style of wines for Austria are like Germany
   b) Austria has a rather low quality wine control system
   c) Much of the wine from Austria are white
   d) Austria makes sweet Riesling style wines.

5) Which of the following is a red grape of Austria?
   a) Furmint
   b) Riesling
   c) Sylvaner
   d) Blaufränkisch

❖ South Africa (Chapter 8)

1) Name 3 Regions in South Africa for wine production
   a) _____
   b) _____
   c) _____

2) In South Africa, another name for Chenin Blanc is:
   a) Shiraz
   b) Steen
   c) Muller Thurgau
   d) Fume Blanc
   e) None of the above

3) Which one of the following varietals is part of the hybrid for Pinotage.
   a) Cabernet Sauvignon
   b) Merlot
   c) Syrah
   d) Cinsuat

4) Which of the following is not a true statement
   a) The majority of wines produced in South Africa are from Co-operatives.
   b) The Palomino is another grape grown in South Africa.
   c) The leading grape varietal in South Africa is Cabernet Sauvignon.
   d) Another name for Sauvignon Blanc in South Africa is Steen.

❖ South America (Chapter9)

1) Name two major region of Chile.
   a) _____
   b) _____

2) Name a popular red grape grown in Chile that was once a well used Bordeaux varietal in France.
   a) _____

3) Name one of the Valley region in the Central Valley of Chile
   a) _____

4) Name two major wine region of Argentina
   a) _____
   b) _____

5) Which of the following is true?
   a) Argentina is the 8th largest wine producing region in the world.
   b) Argentina is mostly known for Pinotage
   c) Argentina is the 5th largest wine producing region in the world.
   d) Argentina is most known for Prosecco.

6) A very popular red grape in Argentina
   a) Tempranillo
   b) Garnacha
   c) Malbec
   d) Nebbiolo

7) Name one region in the North-west part of Chile
   a) _____

8) Name the largest wine producing region in Argentina
   a) _____

❖ Australia (Chapter 10)

1) Name 3 major wine production regions in Australia (State Level)
   a) _____
   b) _____
   c) _____

2) Australia's appellation system is called
   a) Wine of Origin
   b) Australian Viticultural Area
   c) Geographic Indicator
   d) Wine Zones

3) For varietal labeling in Australia, the wine must consist of what percentage of grapes
   a) 75%
   b) 85%
   c) 95%
   d) 100%
   e) None of the above

4) The most planted wine grape in Australia is
   a) Shiraz
   b) Cabernet Sauvignon
   c) Chardonnay
   d) Semillon

5) Coonawarra is known for what type of wines
   a) Dry red wines
   b) Dry white wines
   c) Sweet wines
   d) Sparkling wines

❖ New Zealand (Chapter 11)

1) Which region is on the North Island of New Zealand
   a) Hawke's Bay
   b) Walker Bay
   c) Otago
   d) Nelson

2) The most well known appellation in New Zealand is
   a) Auckland
   b) Gisborne
   c) Marlborough
   d) Martinbourough

3) Popular and well know grape of New Zealand
   a) Chenin Blanc
   b) Chardonnay
   c) Sauvignon Blanc
   d) Cabernet Sauvignon

❖ United States (Chapter 12)

❖ California

1) Name 6 major wine regions of California
   a) _____
   b) _____
   c) _____
   d) _____
   e) _____
   f) _____

2) Which of the following is true
   a) California ranks 4th in wine production for the World
   b) California's leading red grape is Merlot
   c) California's wine laws are the highest caliber in the world
   d) California is exempt from the BATF because of its production levels.

3) List one of the two adopted red grapes for California
   a) _____

4) Labeled with a vintage, the wine must have at least _____% of the <u>year or vintage.</u>

5) Label with the state of California the wine must contain at least what% of that <u>grape variety.</u>
   a) _____

6) Labeled with California what % of the grape must come from the <u>state</u>
   a) _____

7) Labeled with that county what % of the grape must come from that <u>county</u>
   a) _____

8) Labeled with an AVA what % of grape must be come from that <u>AVA</u>
   a) _____

9) AVA stands for:_____

10) The Volstead Act (Prohibition) was enacted
   a) 1918   b. 1920   c. 1933   d. 1927

11) The most planted white grape in California is
   a) _____

12) The most planted red grape in California is
   a) Merlot
   b) Zinfandel
   c) Cabernet Sauvignon
   d) Petite Sirah

❖ Washington

True or False

1) **WWQA**: In 1999 a trade organization was formed to promote the wine industry and set quality standards for the members of the organization.
   a) _____

2) Reserve wines are not to exceed 25% of winery's production or 3,000 cases.
   a) _____

3) 85% of the grapes must come from Washington or the percentage of the source should be listed on the label.
   a) _____

4) Which of the following grape varietals is considered to be more appropriately associated with Washington?
   a) Merlot
   b) Pinot Noir
   c) Malbec
   d) Gewürtraminer

5) The smallest district straddling the Washington / Oregon border.
   a) Puget Sound
   b) Yakima Valley
   c) Walla Walla.
   d) Sonoma Valley

❖ Oregon

True or False

1) Estate wines must be within 5 miles of the winery?
   a) _____

2) State law requires 75% minimum content of whatever grape variety is named on the label?
   a) _____

3) Due to approve appellation recognition Oregon is permitted to use terms such as Champagne, Chablis, and Burgundy on the label of their wines.
   a) _____

4) Which of the following grape varietals is considered to be more appropriately associated with Oregon?
   a) Chenin Blanc
   b) Pinot Noir
   c) Malbec
   d) Pinotage

5) Name two of the major wine growing regions in Oregon.
   a) _____
   b) _____

❖ New York

True or False

1) The majority of wines produced in New York are from Hybrid grapes?
    a) _____

2) Lake Erie AVA is the largest grape growing county outside of California?
    a) _____

3) The Vitis Vinifera accounts for approximately 30% of New York's wine production?
    a) _____

4) New York is much more known for their French varietals, than Hybrid species?
    a) _____

5) Name 3 typical varietals best known in New York
    a) _____
    b) _____
    c) _____

6) Name 2 of the major wine region within New York
    a) _____
    b) _____

7) Name 3 of the major varietals grown in New York
    a) _____
    b) _____
    c) _____

Glossary

Acid: A nature occurrence in wine. Acid gives liveliness and zest to a wine. Proper balance of acid and other components makes for a vibrant and exciting wine.

Aging: The process of having the wine mature. Aging occurs over an extended period of time. Not all wine will benefit nor go through an aging process. The aging process is related typically to barrel and later in bottle.

Alcohol: The product of converting sugar by yeast consumption. The alcohol for wine is in the family of Ethanol or Ethyl alcohol.

Appellation: This term is generally related to a French relationship of recognized and certified region unique in soil composition and boundaries indicating where the grapes come from and made into wine.

Aroma: A term in general used to describe the smell of the wine which is derived from the grapes and aging characteristics.

Autolysis: The decomposition of yeast cells by its own enzymes, basically the consumption of itself. When wine has undergone "sur lie", it experiences this effect and it actually adds other dimensions to the wine.

AVA: This term relates to North America, and defined as American Viticultural Areas. It addresses boundaries and limiting regional factors or characteristic unique to that particular area.

Bacchus: The Roman god of wine.

Balance: A term used to define several components of wine when they are at equilibrium to the other. This is where (Fruit, acidity, alcohol, Tannin and so on) are in harmony without any one component standing out or out doing the other.

Barrel-Fermented: This is a process of actually fermenting the wine in the barrel as oppose to stainless steel tanks or other median.

BATF: A North American acronym for Bureau of Alcohol, Tobacco and firearms: this organization oversees these individual areas in relationship to applicable laws and regulations.

Bentonite: An organic diatom, a type of clay used for clarifying wine by binding suspended solids in the wine and weighting them down to the bottom of the wine vessel.

Biodynamic:

Blended: This technique of combining two or more lots or types of wine is an attempt to enhance flavor, characteristics and complexity in the final product. The intent is to use the best of each varietal's contribution.

Bodega: A Spanish term (word) for winery

Botrytis Cinerea: Known as Noble Rot, is a favorable fungus which dehydrates the grapes by extracting water through the skin of the grape, altering the water to glucose ratio allowing higher sugar content for Must and later sweet wines. Botrytis is not favorable for red grapes.

Bouquet: Refers to the scent of the wine derived from aging and wine making techniques.

Brix: A term used to represent a unit measurement of sugar and potential alcohol typically before harvest and at the time of crush. The measurement gives some indication of the potentially final percentage of alcohol after fermentation.

Cane: A shoot or long stem extending from the vine and as it grows becomes the cane. The cane is pruned annually after each harvest in early part of the following year.

Canopy: The leafy portion of the vine that offers shade to the fruit and provides energy for the entire vine through photosynthesis process.

Cap: After crush and during fermentation the skins and pulp floats to the top of tank while separating from the juice and creates a thick layer of grapes skins, pulp, and stem. The color comes from the skin of the grape and therefore the cap must be punched down repeatedly to main contact with the juice.

Carbon Dioxide: CO_2 this gas is expelled during fermentation in response to the biological function of yeast consuming sugar and producing a CO_2 byproduct. The CO_2 is the event producing bubbles in Champagne or Sparkling wine.

Carbonic Maceration: A type of fermentation in which the use of whole berry clusters is used instead of crushing them. This process creates a fermentation internal to the berry bunches to produce a softer and grapey type of wine. This is for more indigenous to wine and region of Beaujolais.

Cava: A Spanish term for sparkling wines.

Chaptalization: The process of adding sugar to the must to increase potential alcohol and possibly sweetness of the wine.

Clone: To make an identical copy of; is the general definition. In the case of vines, it is the cutting of one vine and planting or cultivating that cutting to produce the exact varietal.

Cold Fermentation: A process used to maintain a cooler or cold temperature during fermentation. This process allows control by use of stainless steel tank with double walls that coolant flows between and is regulated accordingly to desire temperature. This type of fermentation process produces fresh fruit aromas and characteristic of youthful favors.

Cold Stabilization: Or chill proofing is a term and process by which the tartaric acid is encourage to precipitate out of the wine into a crystallize form. Often wine that has not undergone a cold stabilization process and then stored in refrigeration will display crystallized tartaric acid fallout appearing to be broken glass when poured.

Commune: This is typically a small wine growing region surrounding a village.

Cooperage: A facility for making oak barrels. A cooper; is an individual specializing in making oak barrels or containers.

Cordon: A branch stemming from the grapevine in a single or dual manner from which cane or shoot grows out.

Corked: A term that refers to a musty smell associated tainted corks (natural corks), sometimes the term wet dog come mind. This can happen in the forest where the cork is harvested, during the processing of producing the cork or during storage in the bottle. The effect is Trichoroanisole or TCA producing a mold that can be detected in smell.

Crianza: A classification used in Spain to represent the youngest of wine aged in barrels.

Crossing: Marring and producing vines by cross-pollination of two different varietals of the same species, therefore creating a new varietal

Cru: or "Growth" term used for a single area of quality, can be a village or vineyard.

Crush: The process of slightly breaking the skin of a cluster of grape berries to start or expose the juice for fermentation.

Cutting: A section cut from the cane or shoot, that later can be planted or grafted to start another grapevine. See clone.

Decant: To separate the wine from any sediment resting at the bottom of a bottle or decanter.

Demi-Sec: A French term meaning half dry or can be viewed as half sweet. Demi-Sec referred typically in Champagne or sparkling wine.

De-stemmer: A piece of equipment used to separate the stems from a cluster of grapes after harvest and before fermentation.

Disgorging: This is a French term used in the process of removing the spent yeast from the bottle of champagne or sparkling wine. The yeast is ejected out of the bottle after a laborious process of riddling.

Dry: A term used to represent a bottle of wine with little to no residual sugar.

Einzellage: A German term used for a single vineyard.

Eiswein: A German term used for "Ice Wine" made from non botrytised affected grapes that are partially frozen in the vineyard.

Enology: The study of wine making.

Estate Bottled: Wine that is grown on the estate vineyard and bottled at the vineyard or within a regulated and accepted range of the vineyard. This is by most standards 85% to a 100%.

Esters: Aromatic compounds present in the wine due to acid and alcohol molecules binding together during fermentation and aging.

Extra Dry: A French term use to represent a certain level of dryness or sweetness of a champagne or sparkling wine. This term is often confused with expectations of being very dry it is actually somewhat sweet. Extra dry is near the middle of the rating range.

Ethanol / Ethyl Alcohol: a form of alcohol produced by yeast.

Extraction: This term is used in respect to pulling color out of the skin of the grape for a darker and richer wine during fermentation.

Fermentation: The act of converting sugar into alcohol and CO_2, heat is also produce through this biological function of yeast.

Filtering: A mechanical operation of removing sediment, spent yeast and other solids suspended in the wine.

Fining: This process is used to remove suspended solids by adding a clarifying agent such as egg whites or bentonite to the wine. The agent binds with the suspended solid, coagulants and settling to the bottom and the wine. The wine is later racked off.

Finish: This is a term used as an expression to explain the overall fill left in the mouth after tasting the wine. The finish is expressed in terms of long, short or something in between, often said to be smooth or rough, lingering or abrupt.

Flor: A film that builds up on top of Sherry as it ages in the barrel or cask. This can develop to several inches thick and will have a consistency of foamy oatmeal.

Fortified: Wines that undergo the addition of brandy added to the wine to increase the alcohol content. The bandy is clear and odorless as to not affect the wine.

Free Run: The first of the juice released during pressing, actually with little pressing is more accurate.

Grafting: The use of cuttings and attaching it to the rootstock (scion) to produce a single grapevine.

Gran Reserva: A term used in Spain representing long term aging, great vintage, and from a limited amount of the total vineyard.

Grosslage: A German term meaning "Large site". This term in meant for a group of vineyards under one site.

Hybrid: The act of creating a new varietal by merging to separate species together. The typical expectation is the benefiting qualities of both.

Isinglass: This is often used as a fining agent for clarifying wine. It comes from the air bladders of sturgeons mostly but other fish as well.

Late Harvest: Grapes that are allowed to remain on the vine longer than the regular harvest time. This process provides additional time to reach greater Brix levels and ripeness.

Lees: the spent yeast and solids that settle to the bottle of the barrel or tank.

Legs: This is the reaction due to the viscosity (alcohol, glycerol and other complex factors); resulting in thickness, width and speed of wine running down the inside of the glass. Contrary to some belief, the quality of the wine is independent to the legs.

Limestone: A sedimentary rock made of calcium Carbonite.

Macroclimate: The overall weather conditions for a large region for grape growing.

Maderized: Often referred to as being cooked or heated due to the process used to make Madeira which is heated in an oven or oven like vessel called an estufa.

Malolactic Fermentation: A bacterial fermentation process to convert Malic acid to Latic acid as a means to soften the wine and offer rounder edges produced by the harsher Malic acid.

Meritage: A term adopted by the United States when addressing wines that are blended with Bordeaux varietals in the same manner as Bordeaux.

Mesoclimate: The local weather condition of a vineyard.

Microclimate: Related to Mesoclimate but can imply the condition to specific portion of the vineyard or vine.

Must: This is a wine making term used after the crushing the grapes, it is the combination of skin, pulp, seeds, stems and juice.

Negociant: a French term used for the individual acting as a middle man (person) that purchase grapes from vineyards to make wine and market the product.

New World: A term used to represent all countries outside of Europe; North America, South America, Australia, New Zealand, South Africa, etc.

Noble Rot: The good rot, also know as Botrytis Cinerea. This is a mold that attacks the skin of the grapes by dehydrating the grapes through the skin by means of evaporation. This produces sweeter berries by changing the water to sugar ratio. See Botrytis Cinerea.

Nose: The smell of a wine.

Old World: Relegated to Europe and the surrounding Mediterranean basin.

Organic: Vineyards grown without the aid or use of chemical fertilizers, herbicides, pesticides.

Oxidation: The exposure of wine to air. Some wine benefit from some level exposure to air while greater exposure destroys the wine. Sherry is an example of an oxidation process for greater benefit.

pH: A measurement in respect to the ratio of Acid to Alkalinity. The range is from 0 to 14 with 7 being neutral. Most wines fall near 3.5, plus or minus a few tenths.

Phylloxera: a tiny aphid that attacks the vine's Rueda and will destroy the vine over a couple of years.

Pomace: After pressing the result is a compressed form of skins, seeds, stem and pulp, without the juice.

Press: The act of applying pressure to a vat of grapes to extract the juice from the must. There are a number of different types of press.

Pruning: An annually event of cutting the cane back to a couple of inches in preparation for the upcoming season. This can also apply of mid season pruning to cut back on foliage or canopy.

Pulp: The meaty or fleshy part of the grape.

Pump Over: A process during fermentation where the wine is pumped over the cap to provide greater extraction of color and richness of the wine. The process is often done several times a day during the early stages of fermentation.

Punch Down: The opposite of pumping over but still accomplishing the same results, mixing the wine and cap to obtain greater color, flavor and tannin extraction.

Punt: the indentation found at the bottom of the bottle. The punt adds strength to the bottle, especially for sparkling wine under pressure.

Racking: A method to clarify the wine by drawing off the wine from the lees that have settled on the bottom with other solids. Racking may occur several times during the aging process before bottling. With each racking greater clarification is obtained.

Reserve: The is not an official regulated term and mean nothing from a legal aspect in North America but is used to identify wines that have been selected from a recognized portion of the vineyard for better quality and often represents better use of barrels, treatment, limitation of production, etc. Washington State has made as exception to this with their WWQA that does hold greater regard for the used term. European countries do apply regulations and laws for compliance.

Residual Sugar: A certain amount of sugar left in the wine after fermentation is completed.

Riddling: This is a process of encouraging the sediment and spent yeast to the neck of the bottle. This is laborious effort of rotating the wine bottles a quarter turn daily and eventually disgorging the accumulated solid.

Rootstock: The part of the vine that is in the soil. There are many different rootstock varieties and are used in respect to growing and weather condition.

Sec: A French term that is usually confusing, meaning dry but is used to indicate level of sweetness. See demi-sec.

Secondary Fermentation: The fermentation process that takes place in the bottle (Champagne or sparkling wine). This can take place in the tank and then transferred into a bottle as well.

Sediment: the solids that fall out of the suspension state in the wine and eventually settle to the bottom of the barrel or tank.

Sélection des Grains Nobles: Wine from hand sorted over ripe grapes, affected by Botrytis Cinerea.

Shoot: A new grow that stems for the cordon during the growing season of the vine. Shoots will eventually produce leaves and fruit.

Skin Contact: for red wine; the time the wine is physically in contact with the skin of the grapes. This desire is to extract color from the skin for the red wine depth.

Solera: A system used primarily for fortified wine, sherry in particular where various vintages are systematically blended from the oldest vintage to the more recent vintage in order to add uniformity, character and complexity to the new wines.

Sommelier: The person that is responsible for assisting diners in selecting wine with their meals, managing the wine inventory, selection of wines, and wine program for a given restaurant.

Sparkling Wine: a wine that has undergone the process of accumulating bubbles through secondary fermentation such as Champagne.
Spur: A short cane of a few inches, a result from pruning with one or two remaining buds.

Still Wines: A wine without carbonation or effervescence.

Sulfur Dioxide: A common and natural chemical that is used for wine preservation prior to fermentation to prevent bacterial type spoilage and the prevention of the growth of wild yeast.

Sur Lie: The aging of wine on the Lees (spent yeast)

Table wine: A standard still wine, that is dry and moderate in terms of alcohol.

Tannin: a Chemical compound present in the skin of the grape, stem, stalk and pips. This compound is sought when making red wine as a natural preservative. The characteristic are leaving a dry sensation on the gums when present.

Tartaric Acid: One of several acids naturally present in the grapes and additional amounts are often added when lacking in the initial must. The acid is responsible for the liveliness and zest in a wine.

Temperance Movement: the temperance movement began in the mid-1830s promoting moderation rather than abstinence. Not long after a more successful abstinence movement was underway. The movement never really brought about Prohibitio

Terrior: A French term use to describe the soil, climate and all growing conditions contributing to the total essence of the wine's character.

Toasted / Toasting: The charring of the inside and sometime the head of the oak barrels. There are various levels that are categorized into light, medium and heavy toasting.

Topping up: Wine loss in a barrel takes place over a period of time. Topping up is the process of adding additional wine to the barrel to replace air as the wine evaporates. Air is not something you want to remain in the barrel.

Trellis: The support system for the vine, canopy and fruit as the vine continues to grow and produce greater weight.

TTB: a shorten term for "The Alcohol and Tobacco Tax and Trade Bureau".

Ullage: The gap or space existing between the bottom of the cork and the top of the wine in the bottle.

Un-filtered: See filter also. This is the process of not filtering the wine through a mechanical means.

Un-fined: See fining. The process of not fining the wine by use of gelatins, egg whites, Bentonite etc…

Varietal: The unique or specific characteristics the makes the difference between one variety of grape from another. The term or use of varietal and grape are often interchangeable.

Vendage Tardive: A French term used to describe the "Late Harvest" wine of Alsace.

Véraison: A French term used to describe the point when the grape changes color; from green to red.

Viniculture: A term used for the science of wine making but Enology is more common, appropriate and frequently used.

Vintage: A year the wine was harvested.

Viscosity: The characteristic of a wine based on the alcohol, glycerol and other complex factors that gives the wine a consistency ranging from a watery appearance to a thick syrupy quality.

Vitis: The genus of the grapevine within the plant world. There are several Vitis species used to make wine.

Yeast: A single cell organism, use to convert sugar into alcohol. This is the primary means of making wine.

Yield: The amount of grape clusters produce during growing season in the vineyard. This is often restricted based on country and regions that are conforming to established wine laws.

MAPS in the TEXT BOOK

- France
- Bordeaux
- Burgundy
- Rhone Valley
- Italy
- Piedmont
- Tuscany
- Spain / Portugal
- Germany
- Austria
- South Africa
- Chile
- Argentina
- Australia
- New Zealand
- Sonoma
- Napa
- Paso Robles
- Santa Ynez
- Oregon
- Washington
- New York
- ***All wine region maps were provided by VinMaps***

References

- Henderson, Patrick J. and Rex Dellie; About Wine 1st edition 2007 Thomson Delmar Learning
- Kramer, Matt; New California Wine; Running Press 2004
- Robinson, Jancis; The Oxford Companion to Wine; 3rd edition 2006
- Fielden, Christopher in association with Wine & Spirit Education Trust 2005 Exploring the world of wines and Spirits
- Vino Italiano; The Regional Wines of Italy; Bastianich, Joseph and Lynch, David; Clarkson potter/ Publishers New York 2002
- Halliday, James; Wine Atlas of Australia; University of California Press Berkey Los Angeles
- Johnson Hugh; The World Atlas of Wine; fourth addition Simon & Schuster. Mitchell Beazley International limited copyright 94
- MacNeil, Karen; The Wine Bible; Workman Publishing, New York copyright 2001
- Cooper, Michael; The Wine Atlas of New Zealand; Hodder Moa Beckett; copyright 2002.
- Jeffs, Julian; The Wines of Spain; Mitchell Beazley; Copyright 2006
- Baldy, Marian W. PhD; The University Wine Course; published by the Wine Appreciation Guild; copyright 1995
- Halliday, James; Classic Wines of Australia and New Zealand; 3rd Edition; copyright 2002.
- Pinney, Thomas; A History of Wine in America (from the beginnings to Prohibition); Vol 1.; copyright 1989, paperback printing 2007.
- Norman, Remington; The Great Domaines of Burgundy; 2nd edition; copyright 1996; Herny Holt and Co. Inc.
- DK; Eye Witness Companions (Wines of the World); 1st edition; copyright 2004; produced for Dorling Kindersley
- Boidron, Bruno and other Authors; ch Cocks – ed. Feret; Bordeaux and Its Wines; 7th edition; copyright 2004
- Stevenson, Tom; The Sotherby's Wine Encyclopedia; 4th edition; copyright 2005.
- ***All wine region maps were provided by VinMaps***

Index

❖ **Enology and Viticulture (Chapter 2)**

TERMINOLOGY MATCHING

1) K

2) L

3) E

4) R

5) M

6) J

7) Q

8) A

9) P

10) O

11) C

12) F

13) I

14) H

15) S

16) D

❖ **Enology and Viticulture (Chapter 2)**

17) True or False

a) TRUE

b) TRUE

c) TRUE

d) TRUE

e) TRUE

18) Which of the following species of vine does the majority of wine making grapes fall under?

B) Vitis Vinifera

19) Which one of the following is used as a fining agent

D)Bentonite

20) What is added to the Must to start fermentation

C)Yeast

21) Racking is a process by which:

B) The wine is removed off the lees or sediment

22) Tannin is a substance found in

C) The skin and stalks and aids in the preservation of the wine

23) Better suited soils for a vineyard have the following

C) Very good drainage

24) Name the 5 styles of wine

a) White
b) Red
c) Rosé
d) Sparkling
e) Fortified

25) In respect to making red wine, white wines are typically fermented under the following conditions.

C) At a lower temperature than red wine

26) NAME 4 RED GRAPES

Check red grape listing in textbook

27) NAME 4 WHITE GRAPES

Check white grape listing in textbook

28) Vines that are full with large berries and many bunches are better suited for

B) Inexpensive, common wines

29) Which of the following best describe Mediterranean climate

B) Climate with warm summers and mid winters most of the rainfall occurs in winter.

30) The Purpose of Malolactic fermentation is to

C) Decrease the acidity of the in the finished wine

31) Malolactic fermentation is the result of the action of

B) Bacteria

36)

D) Dry

32) Which of the following is the correct list of grapes used to make Champagne

C) Chardonnay, Pinot Meunier, Pinot Noir

33) In terms of Non-Vintage Champagne, which is true for Vintage Champagne
C) The base wines come from a single year

34) Please name three growing conditions that can occur in the vineyards that will allow the process for making sweet wine.
a) Late harvest
b) Botrytis
c) Ice Wine

35) Please list the six typically accepted levels of Champagne or Sparkling wine indicating (Dryness or Sweetness).
a) Extra Brut
b) Brut
c) Extra Dry
d) Sec
e) Demi-Sec
f) Doux

❖ France (Chapter 3)

36) French wine designations are (from the highest quality level to the basic).
A) Vin de table, VDQS, Vin de pays, AOC

37) Name 6 key Regions in France for wine production
a) Bordeaux
b) Burgundy
c) Alsace
d) Loire Valley
e) Champagne
f) Rhone Valley

38) The top rated vineyards in Burgundy is a
A) Grand Cru

39) Please list the five accepted red Bordeaux varietals
a) Cabernet Sauvignon
b) Merlot
c) Cabernet Franc
d) Petit Verdot
e) Malber

40) The grape use to produce Chablis is
D) Chardonnay

41) The grape used to produce Beaujolais is

C) Gamay

42) The Côte d'Or is divided into regions

B) Côte de Nuits and Côte de Beaune

43) Please name the four quality levels used in Burgundy

a) Bourgogne
b) Village
c) Premier Cru
d) Gran Cru

44) The main red grape of the Northern Rhône is

B) Syrah

45) Some say Syrah reaches its peak expression in

D) Hermitage

46) Name 5 Varietals that can be used for Châteauneuf-du-Pape :

RED	WHITE
• Grenache	Grenache blanc
• Syrah	Clairette
• Mourvèdre	Bourboulenc
• Cinsaut	Roussanne
• Muscardin	Picpoul
• Carignan	Picardan
• Vaccarese	Muscat
• Terret Noir	Marsanne

47) Which of the varietals listed is the most planted grape in the Bordeaux region

C) Merlot

48) Wines of Sancerre would use what grape

a) Sauvignon Blanc

49) Which of the following varietals most define the wines from Pomerol

B) Merlot

50) The key soil type noted for Burgundy is:

a) Limestone

51) Which of the following wines is most noted for the use of Carbonic Maceration

C) Beaujolais

52) Which of the following varietals is NOT a noble grape of Alsace
   B) Chardonnay

53) Please name the term use for a late harvest wine produced in Alsace
   a)   Vendange Tardive

54) Which of the following varietals is typically used for dry, un-oaked, white wines with vegetal flavors and high acidity?
   C) Sauvignon Blanc

❖ Italy (Chapter 4)

55) The top level of quality among Italian wines, by law is
   a)   D) DOCG

56) Barbaresco is made from
   a)   D) Nebbiolo

57) The main red grape in Tuscany is
   B) Sangiovese

58) Chianti is made primarily of what grape.
   a)   Sangiovese

59) Name 4 key regions in the North-west area of Italy
   *Barolo
   *Barberesco
   *Barbera d'Alba
   *Ghemme
   *Gattinara
   *Dolcetto
   *Brachetto d'Acqui
   *Asti
   *Cortese di Gavi
   *Moscatto d'Asti

60) Name the fortified wine that is primarily made in Sicily.
   a)   Marsala

61) Name 3 key regions in the North-east area of Italy
   Fruili-Venezia Giulia
   Veneto
   Bardolino
   Recioto di Soave

62) Name two styles of wine made in the Valpolicella region that utilized dried grapes that are placed on straw mats to reduce the water content. The wines are make dry and sweet.

a) Amarone

b) Recioto

63) What is the main grape used in the Valpolicella region for much of the wines.

a) Corvina

64) Name two sub-regions of the Veneto area

Bardolino

*Recioto di Soave

*Valpolicella

65) Name two of Tuscany's most important red wines:

Brunello di Montalcino

Chianti

Chianti Classico

Vino Nobile de Montepulciano

66) Name one of the Fantasy named "Super-Tuscans"

Sassicaia

Ornellaia,

Tignanello

67) Name 3 regions in the Southern area of Italy

Puglia (Apulia)

Campania

Basilicata

Sicily

Sardinia

❖ Spain and Portugal (Chapter 5)

68) Name 5 Regions in Spain for wine production

Galicia

Rias Baixas

Ribeiro

Navarra

Castilla y Leon

Ribero del Duero

Rueda

68) Name the dominant variety in Rias Baixas:

Rioja
Cataluña
Penedés
Priorato
Andalucia
Jerez

69) Name the dominant variety in Rias Baixas:
D) Albariño

70) The main grape for Sherry production is
B) Palomino

71) Name two styles of Sherry
Fino
Manzanilla
Amontillado
Oloroso

72) Name two of the key grapes use for Cava in Spain
Parellada
Macabeo
Xarel-lo

73) Name two key grape varietals most recognized for the wine of Rioja
a) Tempranillo
b) Garnacha

74) Name a key region in the North-West area of Spain
Galicia
Rias Baixas
Ribeiro

75) Which of the following is a true statement?
C) The key soil of the Jerez region is named Albariza

76) Vintage Port is
B) Typically only made in special years, when approved by (committee).

77) The majority of wine that comes from Vinho Verde is
A) White

78) Portuguese viticulture uses grapes
A) Indigenous to Portugal

79) Name two styles of Port (please check with the list given but example are listed)
White Port
Ruby
Tawny
Late Bottle Vintage
Colheita

80) Which of the following varietals is most common for Port (Portugal)
B) Touriga National

❖ Germany (Chapter 6)

81) Name the styles of German QmP wines in term of sweetness ; from the driest to the sweetest:
a) Kabinett
b) Spatlese
c) Auslese
d) Beerenauslese
e) Trockenbeerenauslese

82) Name 5 Regions in Germany for wine production
Ahr
Baden
Franken
Hessische Bergstrasse
Mittelrhein
Mosel
Nahe
Pfalz
Rheingau
Rheinhessen
Saale-Unstrut
Sachsen
Württemberg

83) The most noble variety of German wines is
D) Riesling

84) The German name for Pinot Noir
A) Spätburgunder

85) Most dominate red wine region in Germany
B) Ahr

86) Most noted and recognized wine region of Germany
    D) Mosel

❖ Austria (Chapter 7)

87) Most popular and important grape varietal in Austria
    a) Grüner Veltliner

88) Name two of the major key region of the four for Austria
    a) Lower Austria
    b) Burgenland
    c) Styria
    d) Vienna

89) Which of the following is not likely a varietal for Austria
    B) Trebbiano

90) Which of the following is not a true statement?
    B) Austria has a rather low quality wine control system

91) Which of the following is a red grape of Austria?
    D) Blaufränkisch

❖ South Africa (Chapter 8)

92) Name 3 Regions in South Africa for wine production
    Constantia
    Overberg
    Paarl
    Robertson
    Stellenbosch
    Walker Bay
    Elgin

93) In South Africa, another name for Chenin Blanc is:
    B) Steen

94) Which one of the following varietals is part of the hybrid for Pinotage.
    D) Cinsuat

95) Which of the following is not a true statement
    E) Another name for Sauvignon Blanc in South Africa is Steen.

❖ South America (Chapter9)

96) Name two major region of Chile.
   Aconcagau
   Casablanca
   Maipo
   Central Valley
   Rapel Valley
   Curicó Valley
   Maule Valley

97) Name a popular red grape grown in Chile that was once a well used Bordeaux varietal in France.

98) Carmenère Name one of the Valley region in the Central Valley of Chile
   Rapel Valley
   Curicó Valley
   Maule Valley

99) Name two major wine region of Argentina
   a) Salta
   b) Mendoza
   c) Rio Negro

100) Which of the following is true?
   C) Argentina is the 5th largest wine producing region in the world.

101) A very popular red grape in Argentina
   C) Malbec

102) Name one region in the North-west part of Chile
   Aconcagau
   Casablanca

103) Name the largest wine producing region in Argentina
   a) Mendoza

❖ Australia (Chapter 10)

104) Name 3 major wine production regions in Australia (State Level)
   a) South Australia
   b) New South Wales
   c) Victoria
   d) Western Australia

105) Australia's appellation system is called
      C) Geographic Indicator

106) For varietal labeling in Australia, the wine must consist of what percentage of grapes
      B) 85%

107) The most planted wine grape in Australia is
      A) Shiraz

108) Coonawarra is known for what type of wines
      A) Dry red wines

❖ New Zealand (Chapter 11)

109) Which region is on the North Island of New Zealand
      A) Hawke's Bay

110) The most well known appellation in New Zealand is
      C) Marlborough

111) Popular and well know grape of New Zealand
      C) Sauvignon Blanc

❖ United States (Chapter 12)

California

112) Name 6 major wine regions of California
      Mendocino
      Lake County
      Sonoma
      Napa
      Monterey County
      Central Coast
      Santa Cruz
      Santa Clara
      Mount Harlan
      Carmel Valley
      Chalone
      Sierra Foothills
      Amador County
      El Dorado County
      Southern region

Paso Robles
York Mountain
Edna Valley
Arroyo Grande
Santa Maria
Santa Ynez

113)   Which of the following is true
A) California ranks 4th in wine production for the World

114)   List one of the two adopted red grapes for California
a)   Zinfandel or Petite Sirah

115)   95%

116)   100%

117)   75%

118)   85%

119)   American Viticultural Areas
a)   B) 1920
b)   Chardonnay

120)   The most planted red grape in California is
C) Cabernet Sauvignon

❖ Washington

True or False

121)   **True**

122)   False

123)   True

124)   Which of the following grape varietals is considered to be more appropriately associated with Washington?
A) Merlot

125)   The smallest district straddling the Washington / Oregon border.
C) Walla Walla.

❖ Oregon

True or False

126) True
127) False
128) False
129) Which of the following grape varietals is considered to be more appropriately associated with Oregon?
   B) Pinot Noir
130) Name two of the major wine growing regions in Oregon.
   a) Willamette Valley
   b) Umpqua Valley

❖ New York

True or False

131) True
132) True
133) False
134) False
135) Name 3 typical varietals best known in New York
   Seyval Blanc
   Vignoles
   Riesling
   Pinot Noir
   Chardonnay
   Cabernet Sauvignon
   Gewürztraminer
136) Name 2 of the major wine region within New York
   Finger Lakes
   Hudson River Valley
   Lake Erie
   Long Island

CPSIA information can be obtained
at www.ICGtesting.com
Printed in the USA
LVIC04n2242291014
411188LV00004B/8